£10

D1626579

THE MARQUES OF COVENTRY

A History of the City's Motor Industry

Brian Long

WARWICKSHIRE BOOKS

First published in Great Britain in 1990 by Warwickshire Books
Copyright © 1990 Brian Long
ISBN 1 871942–02–0

All rights reserved. No part of this publication may be reproduced, stored in a retrieval system, or transmitted in any form or by any means, electronic, mechanical, photocopying, recording or otherwise, without prior permission to the copyright holder.

British Library Cataloguing-in-publication Data
Long, Brian
    The Marques of Coventry: a history of the city's motor industry.
    1. Great Britain. Motor vehicle industries, history
    1. Title
    338.4762920941

Typesetting P & M Typesetting Ltd, Exeter
Printed and bound in Great Britain by BPCC Wheatons Ltd, Exeter

WARWICKSHIRE BOOKS
Official Publisher to Warwickshire County Council

An imprint of Wheaton Publishers Ltd
A member of Maxwell Communication Corporation plc

Wheaton Publishers Ltd
Hennock Road, Exeter, Devon EX2 8RP
Tel: 0392 74121: Telex 42794 (WHEATN G)

SALES
Direct sales enquiries to Warwickshire Books at the address above

Photographs
The publishers wish to thank the following organizations and individuals for their kind permission to reproduce their photographs on the pages indicated:

All Sport: 33; Alvis Ltd: 53 (bottom); Auto Forge Autos: 38; Colin Bartlam: 21 (top left); Birmingham City Museum and Art Gallery: 104 (bottom right); Simon Bishop, Association of Singer Owners: 83 (top); Grahame Bryant 97 (top); Coventry City Library: 1, 2 (right), 4 (top & bottom), 5, 6 (top), 8 (top), 11 (bottom), 12 (bottom), 19 (bottom), 23 (bottom), 46 (left), 74 (middle), 79 (top), 82 (bottom), 83 (bottom left), 99 (top right), 100 (right), 101 (top), 102 (top); Coventry City Council: 3 (left), 45 (bottom), 105 (bottom right); The Donington Collection: 31 (middle); Arthur Glover: 18; Gillian Goodall: 84; Ted Hewitt: 25 (top); Jaguar Cars Ltd: 7, 10 (top), 89 (left), 91, 92, (top & bottom), 93 (top & bottom), 94 (bottom), 95 (top & bottom), 99 (bottom), cover (middle); Kalmar (UK) Ltd: 105 (left), 116 (top); Brian Long: 9 (top middle), 21 (top right), 28, 31 (left & right), 35 (bottom), 37 (bottom), 45 (top right), 46 (right), 50 (bottom), 59, 62 (top), 67 (top), 68, 69, 70 (left & right), 71, 81 (top), 82 (top left & right), 86 (top), 88 (bottom), 89 (left), 94 (top), 98, 106 (top left & right), 108 (left & right), 115 (bottom right); Marendaz Special Register: 30 (middle); Midland Air Museum: 111, 112 (bottom), 113 (top & bottom), 115 (top), 116 (bottom); Motor Panels Ltd: 99 (top left), 107; Motor Magazine: 80 (top); Museum of British Motor Transport, Coventry: 6 (bottom), 8 (middle & bottom), 9 (top), 19 (top), 24 (middle), 25 (middle), 29 (top), 30 (middle), 36, 41 (top & middle), 45 (top left), 47, 50 (top), 54 (right), 55 (bottom), 60, 61 (top), 66, 67 (bottom), 76 (bottom), 80 (bottom), 90 (bottom), 100 (left), 102 (top), 105 (top right), 109 (top); National Motor Museum, Beaulieu: 11 (top), 12 (bottom) 13, 14 (top), 19 (top & bottom), 22, 23 (top), 24 (top & bottom), 24-25 (bottom), 26, 29 (bottom), 30 (top & bottom), 31 (top), 34, 35 (top), 37 (top), 40, 54 (left), 83 (bottom right), 87 (bottom), cover (top); National Motorcycle Museum: 104 (top, middle & bottom right); Patrick Collection: 90 (bottom); Peugeot-Talbot Ltd: 72, 73 (top & bottom), 75, 76 (top), 79 (middle & bottom), 86 (bottom), 87 (top & middle), 88 (top), 110; Terry Phillips, Park Sheet Metal: 50 (middle); Maurice Ponder: 74 (top); Post Vintage Humber Car Club: 77 (top & bottom), 78 (top & bottom), 109 (bottom); A. B. Price Ltd: 14 (bottom), 15 (top & bottom), 16 (right); Proton Cars (UK): 96; Quadrant Photo Library: 22, 44; Raoul Raymondiss 97 (bottom); John Ridley: 9 (bottom middle); Riley Register Bulletin Editor's Collection: 55 (top), 56 (top & bottom), 57 (top & bottom), 58 (top, middle & bottom), 103; Rolls-Royce Heritage Trust: 39, 41 (bottom), 42, 43 (top & bottom), 106 (bottom), 112 (top), 114; Mr Simmons, Red Triangle Services: 51 (top & bottom), 52 (top & bottom), 53 (top), 115 (bottom left), cover (bottom); Brian Smith: 9 (bottom); Standard Motor Club: 61 (bottom), 62-3 (bottom), 63 (top), 64 (top), 65; Les Vincent: 64 (bottom); Vivi Cycles: 101 (bottom); Phil Warren: 37 (middle); A. N. Weaver: 21; John Wright Photography: 21 (top left); Daniel Young: 48 (top & bottom), 49.

The publishers have made every effort to trace the copyright holders of all the photographs in this book.

FOREWORD

This book, *The Marques of Coventry*, is a remarkable history of the car, cycle and motorcycle industries of the city from the 'bone-shakers' of the 1860s right through to the cars that will take Coventry well into the 1990s.

The detailed information that the author has provided concerning the early history of the companies involved, including those which have long since ceased to exist, far exceeds what one would have thought possible after such a long period of time.

Having been personally associated for over fifty years with one of the companies with which he deals (Alvis), I thought I knew all there was to know about it, but I was much further enlightened by Mr Long's book.

He is to be congratulated on his efforts, for the publication is one that those interested in the subject cannot afford to be without.

I look forward to him writing a sequel recording the achievements of the city's many designers and engineers, without whose talents, Coventry would have remained a small provincial town.

Arthur F. Varney, C.Eng., F.I.Mech.E., F.R.Ae.S.

ACKNOWLEDGEMENTS

I should like to thank all the staff at the Museum of British Road Transport in Coventry, the archive staff at the National Motor Museum, Beaulieu, the many enthusiasts at the Midland Air Museum, Baginton, John Ward at the Patrick Collection, Birmingham, the National Motorcycle Museum, Birmingham, and of course the Coventry Libraries and City Records Office. Much help in the way of photographs has also come from many owners' clubs.

The photographic departments at both Peugeot-Talbot and Jaguar Cars have, as always, been most helpful. To Major Tony Rolt and John Braithwaite of FF Developments, Terry Phillips of Park Sheet Metal, Anthony Gough of Kalmar UK, J.S.F. Grindlay of CMS, Mr Simmons of Red Triangle Services, Elaine West of Alvis, David Watson of Motor Panels, and Barry Price of A.B. Price – many thanks for your help and support.

Many individuals, such as Tony Freeman, Lee Thomas, Arthur Glover, Gillian Goodall, Ray Cook, Bill Smith, Ernie Newbold, Tony Bird, John Ridley, Stephen Lewis, Maurice Ponder, A.N. Weaver, Graham Bosworth, John Eales, Andy Rouse, John McGuire, Roger Morris, Ted Hewitt, and of course Arthur Varney, have all helped along the way. My thanks also to Ian Mobley for his help with the photographs, and to Cheylesmore Garage for supplying the Peugeots shown on p.88. I know for sure that I have left out many names, so please accept my apologies – I shall know in future to keep a record!

Last, but certainly not least, I wish to thank the publishers, for without them, there would be no book.

Brian Long

CONTENTS

AN INTRODUCTION TO COVENTRY'S INDUSTRIAL HERITAGE

COVENTRY HAS BEEN A MANUFACTURING CITY SINCE THE MIDDLE AGES. BY THE START OF THE NINETEENTH CENTURY, LOCAL FACTORIES WERE HEAVILY COMMITTED TO THE HIGHLY SKILLED TRADES OF WATCH-MAKING AND THE TEXTILE INDUSTRY.

It was around 1820 that the birth of the popular cycle was witnessed in the United Kingdom. This earliest machine would be known as the 'hobby-horse'. Developments were very slow in the beginning, but towards the latter half of the century, the cycle's potential was at last realized.

The gradual decline of the textile business during the 1860s led to the need for other work. Fortunately for the city, a young man by the name of Rowley Turner rode into Coventry on his early 'bone-shaker' bicycle. He had come to persuade his uncle, Josiah Turner, to build 400 of these machines. Josiah agreed; thus a whole new industry was born.

Turner's firm, the Coventry Sewing Machine Co., was re-formed into the Coventry Machinists Co. in order to fulfill young Rowley's request. The factory would become the home of the Swift Cycle Co. when they acquired the ailing business in 1896.

The foreman of Swifts in those early days was a certain James Starley, 'the father of the safety cycle', as he will always be remembered. Starley continued to improve the machines, feeding other smaller concerns with fresh approaches to their development. The Ariel 'penny farthing', one of the more notable cycles of the time, was actually patented by Starley and William Hillman. Hillman was just one of many who would later go on to concentrate on building automobiles.

H.J. Lawson (another name that will crop up from time to time) invented the chain-driven safety cycle in 1874. He offered the manufacture to the newly formed BSA (Birmingham Small Arms) company, but – amazingly – they declined. It was John Kemp Starley (nephew of James) who, in the mid-1880s, led the industry to the safety cycle as we know it today.

By 1897, a slump had set into this trade, brought about by a vast over-investment. Many companies were forced either to close, or to revert back to their original business. Some, though, decided to invest in future forms of transport, notably the motor car. Such famous marques as Rover, Singer, Hillman, Humber, Sunbeam and Lea-Francis would become household names in the not so distant future. From being the cycle-building capital of the world, Coventry's importance in the transport trade grew still more in the following years.

The automobile, like the cycle, is a difficult invention to credit to any one person. It would be fairer to say that it came about through a series of evolutionary processes, rather than simply arriving on the scene.

Nicolas Cugnot was responsible for the first recognized vehicle that actually worked. This was a steam wagon built in France, and completed in 1769. In England, the development of road vehicles was always restricted, especially when the Red Flag Act of 1865 was enforced, limiting machines to a maximum of 4 m.p.h., and requiring a man to walk in front of them, carrying a warning flag.

By this time, foreign inventors were well ahead in the development stakes. Nikolaus Otto was the first person to introduce the four-stroke engine, ready for the likes of Gottlieb Daimler and Karl Benz to give the world the rudimentary internal-combustion engine.

In the late 1880s, F.R. Simms, a young mechanical engineer, attended an exhibition in Bremen. It was here that he saw the single vertical-cylinder internal-combustion engine, the invention of Gottlieb Daimler and his partner William Maybach.

Simms and Daimler became good friends, and by 1893 Simms had founded the Daimler Motor Syndicate in this country, having acquired the patent rights of the Daimler engine for the United Kingdom. The obvious location for the development of the company was Coventry, because Simms knew that mechanical skills and inventiveness abounded within the city.

The famous Emancipation Run of 1896 opened up a whole new incentive for a British industry. Many firms entered into the trade, though most failed to succeed for long. During the same year, a financial group known as the British Motor Syndicate purchased the Daimler Motor Syndicate, along with the Daimler Motor Co. Ltd, which Simms was in the process of forming. It was in this year that the assembly of the first British Daimlers started. By the following year, series production was well under way. When the Prince of Wales bought a Coventry-built Daimler in 1900, this gave the industry a much-needed boost, as well as a large gain in respectability.

The natural progression from cycle- to motorcycle production didn't really happen until the turn of the century, but Coventry's fame, created by the established cycle trade and the new motor trade, brought many other companies and skilled engineers into the city.

Tricars proved to be a popular mode of transport during the early 1900s, but, with the introduction of pneumatic tyres, and the adoption of frontal engines and bonnets, which brought the 'horseless-carriage' look to an end, the development of the car came on in leaps and bounds.

Mechanical and technical refinement continued throughout the Edwardian era, and some of the most beautiful automobile creations came from this time. It wasn't all plain sailing, though. For instance, Daimler found themselves in financial trouble, and were acquired by the BSA group. Larger vehicles were taxed heavily from 1910, but this did at least lead to the development of the 'light car', after the 'cyclecar' had put in a brief appearance. Light cars were basically miniature versions of the larger prototypes, but with their engine capacity limited to 1.5 litres. Not only were they more comfortable than, and technically far superior to, the cyclecar, but, with prices usually under £250, they became very popular and quickly found a market.

By the start of the First World War, Coventry was producing around a third of Britain's total car output, and this included many of the industry's most prestigious names.

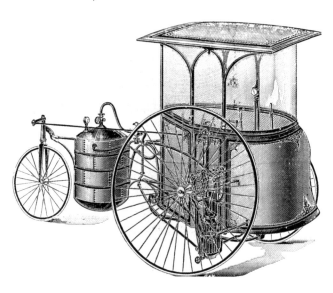

The original caption reads: 'THE FIRST PETROLEUM MOTOR CAR – Invented by H.J. Lawson'. This was certainly not the first petrol-engined vehicle, although it may well have been built to a Lawson design!

Fleet Street, Coventry, soon after the turn of the century

Many other local companies enjoyed a good reputation for bodies, engines and other components supplied to the trade. This concentrated flow of energy, directed straight at its car industry, made the city almost unique.

The immediate post-war boom attracted even more new firms into the industry, but the depression of 1921 didn't help the trade. Many companies, and not just the newly formed ones, were forced out of business. Despite this, several famous marques were formed at the time, and mass production was introduced into some of the larger concerns.

The following years saw many important mergers. These had the effect of spreading the companies' overheads, and thus brought down the prices of their products. Clément–Talbot and Darracq joined forces in the early twenties, followed by Morris and Wolseley in 1927, and the formation of the Humber-Hillman group came just a year later. The massive Rootes empire would also have a say in the very near future.

The British motor trade was once again booming, and by the late 1930s the United Kingdom was second only to the U.S.A. in terms of the production and export of cars and commercial vehicles. In 1937, less than 5 per cent of new cars sold on the home market were of foreign origin, British cars being shielded by tariff protection. Falling car prices (following the advent of mass-production methods) together with generally higher wages helped to bring motoring to a wider public.

The two world wars played a large part in Coventry's development. In 1936 the city became closely involved in the rearmament programme. William Rootes, John Black and Alfred Herbert met Whitehall officials to plan for the building of 'shadow factories' for reserve production in the event of war. The eventual volume production of military equipment had the effect of confirming Coventry as one of the country's leading centres of modern engineering.

The threat of war brought about a marked acceleration in building activities as existing factories were extended, and new ones were built, to accommodate the growth of production. Although many Coventrians enlisted, the city's population still grew, as people would travel for miles to gain employment.

Coventry's role in the Shadow Factory Scheme was only a small part of its response to the war effort. Indeed, the city became a hive of engineering activity. This left it perfectly poised for further rapid growth in the immediate post-war era.

Despite a distinct lack of raw materials, and many vehicles going abroad, the period from the post-war years to the mid-1960s was one of considerable success for the British motor industry. Output expanded, jobs were plentiful, and new markets were cultivated. Unfortunately for the city, however, companies were pressed into developing new manufacturing capacity in areas of high unemployment, far away from the traditional heart of the industry in the Midlands. In spite of all this, Coventry continued to be a 'boom town'.

Coventry was particularly badly bombed during the war, and many homes and factories were destroyed

France, Germany and Japan were by now beginning to overtake the British producers in terms of output, and when the sixties drew to a close, the post-war boom was well and truly over – competition was being increasingly felt. This is highlighted by the fact that by 1975 most of the cars sold on the home market were imported. In an attempt to save both Chrysler and British Leyland, the Government had had to step in. These were indeed bad times.

Now only a few car factories remain, and the glory that once belonged to the city may never return, but Coventry has always been at the heart of the British road transport industry. Right from the start, the motor industry played a major part in the city's development and prosperity, and this book outlines the history of every single car-manufacturing company ever to be based within the shadows of the Three Spires.

THE LAWSON EMPIRE

HARRY LAWSON HAD GRAND IDEAS OF A BRITISH
MOTOR MANUFACTURING MONOPOLY. THE PROB-
LEMS CAME WHEN HE TRIED TO BUILD HIS
EMPIRE.

> **Great Horseless Carriage Co. Ltd,** *Drapers Field,*
> *1896–1898*
> **Motor Manufacturing Co. (MMC),** *Drapers Field,*
> *1898–1907*
> **Daimler,** *Drapers Field, 1896–*
> **Pennington,** *Drapers Field, Sandy Lane, 1896*
> **New Beeston,** *Quinton Road, 1898*
> **Beeston,** *Quinton Road, 1899*
>
> *Also included:*
> **Garrard and Blumfield,** *1894*
> **British Motor Co,** *Hertford Street, 1896*
> **British Motor Traction,** *Fleet Street, 1906–1910*
> **Lanchester,** *Sandy Lane, 1931–1954*

Harry J. Lawson, inventor of the safety cycle and pioneer of the motor industry in Coventry

Harry Lawson's first links with Coventry were with the cycle industry – in fact, he has been credited as the inventor of the safety cycle as we know it today. Lawson was heavily involved with several cycle-building firms within the city, as well as component suppliers. He was chairman of both the Beeston Tyre Rim Co. and the Beeston Pneumatic Tyre Co., the latter's product being known as the 'New Beeston Tyre'.

Later on, a few quite successful tricycles and quadricycles were built under the marque name of **New Beeston**, making use of the newly acquired De Dion patents. The same sort of vehicles were marketed under the **Beeston** name, although one 3½-h.p. light car was exhibited by Beeston at the 1899 National Cycle Show.

Lawson was not only an engineer but something of a financial expert. When he saw how the automobile trade was developing abroad, he decided to buy as many established patents as possible, thus gaining royalties from any engineering company who used them in the United Kingdom.

Pennington was a wild American inventor who managed to sell his manufacturing rights to Lawson. This was said to have cost him £100000, as well as a storey of the Coventry 'Motor Mills', which were assigned to Pennington himself. The

This Pennington Victoria from around 1895 was almost certainly the only one ever seen in Britain, and may have been brought over from the U.S.A.

THE MOTOR MILLS, COVENTRY,

Represented in the above illustration, is

THE LARGEST AUTOCAR FACTORY IN THE WORLD.

Of the four floors of the building, **Three Floors,** giving a floor space of over **70,000 square feet,** are now being fitted up with the latest and most approved machinery for the manufacture of

AUTOCARS

UNDER THE

PENNINGTON, DAIMLER, AND BOLLEE SYSTEMS.

Most of the machinery is now in position, driven by two 350 h.p. engines, and at work upon the completion of several entirely new designs in autocars, upon which a staff of some

TWO HUNDRED HIGHLY-SKILLED WORKMEN

is now engaged by

THE GREAT HORSELESS CARRIAGE CO., LTD.

Head Offices: 40, Holborn Viaduct, London, E.C.   **Works: Motor Mills, Coventry.**

Publicity was a priority for any company with which Lawson was involved. This is a period advertisement for the Great Horseless Carriage Co.

three-wheeled **Pennington** Torpedo was the first, and indeed the last, result of this unlikely team. One had been entered in the famous Lawson-organized Emancipation Run in 1896, but pulled out when one of its 'unburstable' pneumatic tyres went pop! Only around five of these vehicles with Humber frames were built.

The **Garrard & Blumfield** rights were also owned by Harry Lawson. Garrard & Blumfield had been building electric-powered vehicles in Coventry since 1894, though just how many were produced is not certain.

The British Motor Syndicate Ltd, of which Lawson was chairman, was formed to promote the development and manufacture of the motor car, and soon owned around seventy important patents, one of them being that of the Daimler engine.

Daimler can justly claim to have been the first company in England set up for the sole purpose of manufacturing petrol-driven motor vehicles on a large scale. In fact, the company was founded ten months before the motor car could be used legally on the public highway.

The story begins in 1896, when the **Great Horseless Carriage Co. Ltd** was founded. This company was one of a series formed by H.J. Lawson, who still had ideas of obtaining a monopoly of the British automobile industry. The company managed to lease part of a factory owned by the Coventry Cotton Spinning and Weaving Co. but unfortunately records show that very few, if indeed any, vehicles ever left the factory before it closed down.

The Gottlieb Daimler patents licence had previously been passed to the British Motor Syndicate, who, encouraged by the British Motor Manufacturing Co., produced a number of 'MMC' cars. The **Motor Manufacturing Co.** of 1898 was basically a reorganized Great Horseless Carriage Co., and it was headed by George Iden.

Initially, MMC followed two lines of development: first, there were the Daimler-based cars, and then the MMC-built De Dion-engined motorcycles and quadricycles. By 1899, Iden had designed a new series of cars. They had rear-mounted horizontal two-cylinder engines, and were of various sizes, the 4½-h.p. Princess two-seater being the smallest, followed by the Sandringham phaeton, with the 11-h.p. Balmoral charabanc topping the range.

By 1901, MMC had discontinued the rear-engined cars, and reverted back to mounting the engine at the front of the vehicle. The larger cars were closely designed along Panhard lines, although the following year, another new range was introduced, in an attempt to use interchangeable parts. The models now consisted of a 5½-h.p. single-cylinder, an 8-h.p. twin, and a 12-h.p. four-cylinder vehicle. Although these cars were much lower than their predecessors, they still looked rather ungainly, with their large, gilled-tube radiators. At this time, MMC were supplying over thirty companies with their engines, as it was often cheaper for the smaller concerns to buy them from an outside supplier rather than try to build and develop their own.

For 1903, the four-cylinder model was upgraded to a 20-h.p. one (sometimes referred to as the 25 h.p.), and a superb long-wheelbase example of this vehicle was shown at the Paris Salon during the same year.

The Garrard & Blumfield electric brake

Still a very active machine despite its years, this 1898 Daimler can be spotted at outdoor events throughout the year. It is fitted with an MMC engine, and belongs to the Museum of British Road Transport in Coventry's city centre.

In December 1903 Iden resigned from the company, and went on to build his own cars in Fleet Street, so there was little change to the 1904 models. MMC moved out from the Motor Mills late in 1905, and set up across town at Parkside. Here they advertised a large range of cars, from a 9-h.p. single-cylinder right through to a 30/35-h.p. four-cylinder model. Very few (if any) Parkside-built MMC cars ever made it to the market-place, though. A couple of years later the company was revived, and moved down to London. Only experimental cars were to appear in the future. One final reorganization led to a totally new company, retaining only the MMC name, being established in Finchley, but its sole function was to sell, rather than to produce, cars.

It was between January and February 1897 that the first of the Coventry-built Daimlers were completed, built in the Motor Mills that by now the company had acquired and converted for series production; the rest of the building was still being sublet to other Lawson concerns. Within the year, Daimler was already proving itself. The first John O'Groats to Land's End run was accomplished in a car of the marque

1900 Daimler Wagonette

driven by Henry Sturmey, the editor of *Autocar* magazine. As a personal friend of Lawson's, he would have a great influence on the company's success. Another machine reached the summit of the Malvern Beacon, driven by the Hon. Evelyn Ellis, the gentleman who brought the first Daimler-engined Panhard into the country.

Daimler, with their reputation for high-powered and expensive cars, did in the earlier days develop a pioneering version of the light car. Introduced in 1899, it was called the Critchley, after the then works manager. It sold well, and was held in high regard, but it was never meant to be a major part of the company's production activity. In fact, it was initially built purely to use up a surplus of fifty engines supplied by the German Daimler works in Cannstatt. Except for a small 7-h.p. car produced in 1904, of which very few were built, Daimler would stick to the prestige market.

H.R.H. the Prince of Wales (later Edward VII) was given his first ride on the public roads in mid-1898, and in June 1900, after the outstanding success of the Daimlers in the Thousand Miles Trial at the turn of the century, ordered his first Daimler car – the first of many royal Daimlers.

The next major milestone in the company's history was the formation of the Daimler Motor Co. (1904) Ltd. It was in 1904 that the famous fluted grille made its debut; it would be a feature of almost every vehicle produced by the company thereafter. By this time, it was easy to see that one of Daimler's most significant contributions to the Coventry motor industry was a source of experienced manpower. In addition to this, many companies relied on the supply of Daimler components to build their own vehicles.

The **British Motor Traction Co.** had been set up by Selwyn F. Edge, the famous Australian racing cyclist, in 1900. His intention was to carry on the Lawson monopoly of the British motor trade. Indeed, the business was a reconstruction of the British Motor Co., which was itself a reconstruction of the British Motor Syndicate. The **British Motor Co.** was floated in June 1896, with the issue of 175000 shares at £1 each. Cars, motorcycles, vans, motor carts, an omnibus and even motor launches were shown in the company's sales brochure, though it is very doubtful whether anything was ever produced. In 1907, Edge managed to acquire a number of the Lawson-owned patents, including those of De Dion and Mercedes, but little came of the purchases.

During the early part of 1909, work began on the production of a 15-h.p. engine of the revolutionary sleeve-valve 'Silent Knight' type. The designer, an American named Charles Knight, had set himself the task of designing valve-gear that would be far quieter in operation than the 'poppet' type, and so came the Daimler sleeve-valve engine.

In the same year, Dr Frederick W. Lanchester was appointed consulting engineer for the company, and his full life history can still be traced in Coventry at the Lanchester Polytechnic. This extraordinary engineer was also responsible for the Lanchester cars described later on in this chapter.

In 1910 came the amalgamation of the BSA and Daimler interests, which led to the formation of the Daimler Co. Ltd. By 1916, many vehicles had graced the company's catalogues, but the First World War was in full swing, and production was wholly confined to war-work up until 1920, when three chassis from before the war were reintroduced.

1924, and a new 35-h.p. chassis was marketed. Also, for the first time, four-wheel braking was introduced in the Daimler range. An important change was made to the sleeve-valve engines, too. Previously, the sleeves had been made of cast iron but now they were to be machined from steel. It was found that not only did this reduce weight, but the sleeves could be made appreciably thinner, thus increasing the cylinder bore, which in turn raised the power output. During the war, King George's fleet of vehicles, which started service in 1910, had seen much hard wear and tear. They were replaced by four new vehicles sporting the modified engines.

For many years Daimler had been exclusively building six-cylinder engines, but in 1926, the company decided to build a luxury car whose engine should attain a degree of sweetness, silence and absence of vibration never previously achieved with the internal-combustion engine. Obviously, the number of cylinders used was a matter of supreme importance; the twelve-cylinder, 7.1-litre Double-Six was born.

The Double-Six engine was made up of two blocks of six cylinders, each having its own fuel and ignition equipment, but operating on a common crankshaft. The car was gigantic, but its refinement was described as being in a class of its own.

Around a year later, a smaller version of the Double-Six was placed on the market. The engine size was nearly half that of its bigger brother, but none the less King George's fleet of Daimlers were converted to take this new engine.

The adoption of the 'fluid flywheel' came later on. This involved a combination of the epicyclic preselective gearbox and a hydraulic drive. This method of transmission had a massive advantage over the orthodox gearbox for many years, even though a certain amount of criticism was levelled at it in the first instance.

It was in 1931 that the **Lanchester** Motor Co. Ltd was absorbed into Daimler. Lanchester was of course responsible for the first ever petrol-driven four-wheel car actually built in the United Kingdom.

Dr F.W. Lanchester was born in 1868. He had his first car on the road, albeit illegally, in 1895, and soon formed a car-building syndicate. The vehicles incorporated many novel features, a lot of them being years ahead of their time. By

This motor drag was one of the many vehicles illustrated in the British Motor Carriage and Cycle Co.'s brochure.

One of the very early Lanchesters

Daimler has always been a marque supported by royalty. Shown here (outside Coventry's new cathedral) is Queen Mary's 1935 Double-Six. The original V12 engine was later replaced with a smaller, six-cylinder engine to conserve fuel.

A superb Daimler landaulette (c.1915), with coachwork by Hooper

Lanchester Ten with coachwork by Avon of Warwick (1934)

The very last surviving Sprite (and therefore the last Lanchester), seen here with its present owner, Briar Ridley

The 1955 Golden Zebra: one of Lady Docker's exotic Daimlers

1899, the Lanchester Engine Co. had been founded in Birmingham, and just two years later, the first of the Lanchester cars were being sold on a commercial basis.

In 1909 Lanchester resigned from his own company, but decided to remain as a consultant. He would also be called in as an independent consultant by such companies as Daimler, though at this stage there was no other link.

The Lanchester Forty and Straight-Eight are probably the best-known cars built before the takeover, but the marque will always be highly respected for its fine engineering skills.

When the company was acquired by BSA in 1931, work was already at an advanced stage on the new 15/18 chassis. For a while, George Lanchester (Frederick's brother) worked with Laurence Pomeroy to produce the vehicle with a Daimler fluid flywheel, but George later went to work for Alvis. The model had at least one claim to fame, when one was driven to victory in the first ever (1932) RAC Rally. But, except for the loyal few who forced Daimler to badge several of its luxury models as Lanchesters, the marque soon lost some of its high standing, and was often looked upon as the poor relation.

The Lanchester Ten would have been quite successful, but the weight of the machine, combined with a general lack of power, lost crucial sales. The Fourteen was also over-shadowed by its counterparts, the Daimler Conquest immediately stealing the limelight.

The 1954 Sprite was to be the last vehicle with the Lanchester grille. Only a handful were ever built, and indeed, only one example now remains. The marque name was never used again, although Ford did approach Jaguar (the current owners) about the possibility of building Jaguars under licence in Germany. They proposed calling the cars Lanchesters, but perhaps fortunately, the idea was rejected.

Inspired by a 1934 sleeve-valve Pomeroy production of a straight-eight engine, in 1936 the Daimler engineers set about building a redesigned, larger poppet-valved engine. The result was a 4½-litre Straight-Eight, built to such a pitch of perfection, that this engine became a landmark in the history of the British motor industry. A smaller, 3.4-litre version was built later on in the year.

For 1939, the Daimler Fifteen was fitted with a new 18-h.p. engine. The new vehicle was thus designated the 'DB18'. Production continued after the war, though the model was then more commonly known as the 2½-litre saloon. Many desirable vehicles were based on this chassis.

Sir Bernard Docker joined the board in July 1940. His father had been a director before him, and kept a great interest in the company's activities until his death in 1944. It was Sir Bernard's wife, Lady Docker, who put forward the ideas for those outrageously finished 'Docker Daimlers'.

Although Daimler had already been manufacturing motor cars, buses, ambulances, vans, lorries, and engines for both tanks and aeroplanes during the Second World War, the main factory was also responsible for building armoured scout cars. In addition, many components were made, running into millions, for Rolls-Royce and Bristol aero-engines. Many large and small armaments were also produced in both the main and satellite (shadow) factories. Over the war period, Daimler would purchase, among

4½-litre Daimler DK400 with coachwork by Hooper

The Daimler SP250, sometimes known as the Dart, was powered by a 2½-litre V8 engine and had a fibreglass body, which gave it an excellent power-to-weight ratio.

others, the two famous coach-building companies, Hooper and Barker.

Daimler's fiftieth birthday came in 1946. At the Savoy Hotel, a Jubilee Luncheon was held to celebrate this momentous occasion, and in proposing a toast to the company, Lord Brabazon of Tara stated that Daimler, from its small beginnings, had become a national institution.

Several more flamboyant Daimlers were produced by Hooper in the immediate post-war years, notable models being the 'Green Goddess' run of cars and the show-stopping 'Docker Daimlers' of the early fifties.

By the end of the decade, however, Daimler were in serious financial trouble. Sir Bernard was asked to step down from the chairmanship after allegations of extravagance and mismanagement. The company lost its royal patronage, and its range of cars often competed with each other on the new-car market.

The final 'real' Daimlers were the Majestic range and the SP250 sports car, as, in mid-June 1960, Jaguar purchased the Daimler name and business from BSA, along with the factory at Radford, thus allowing Jaguar's production facilities to expand substantially. It cost Jaguar £3.4 million.

The history of the company obviously followed very closely that of Jaguar from then on, but the Daimler marque still lives on today as one of the very few survivors from the early days. The Daimler is marketed as a badge-engineered top-of-the-range Jaguar saloon model, but there is also a very attractive Daimler limousine in its own right – the DS420.

3

IN THE SHADOWS OF THE THREE SPIRES

THE STORY OF THE COMPANIES ONCE BASED IN AND AROUND COVENTRY'S CITY CENTRE.

Raglan, Raglan Street, 1899
Lady, Ford Street, 1899
Endurance, Gosford Street, 1899–1901
Billings, Coventry, 1900
Centaur, West Orchard, 1900–1905
Whitley, Crow Lane, 1900–1905
Ryley, Crow Lane, 1901–1902
Ridley, Upper Well Street, 1901–1904
Forman, High Street, 1901–1911
Aurora, Norfolk Street, 1903
Hamilton, Dale Street, 1903–1910
Hobart Bird, St Patrick's Road, 1904–1910
Iden, Fleet Street, 1904–1907
Lea-Francis, Lower Ford Street, 1904–1960
Climax, George Street, 1905–1907
Dalton & Wade, Spon Street, 1906–1910

Hubbard, Much Park Street, 1906–1910
Doherty, Upper Well Street, 1906–1910
Arno, Gosford Street, 1908–1911
Titan, Carmelite Road, 1911–1912
Glover, Spon Street, 1912–1913
Crouch, Bishop Street, 1912–1928
Rudge, Crow Lane, 1912–1913
Broadway, Coventry, 1913
Taylor-Swetnam, Coventry, 1913
Williamson, Coventry, 1913–1916
Alpha, Gosford Street, 1914–1926/30
Dawson, Priory Street, 1919–1921
Barnett, High Street, 1921–1930
Cluley, Well Street, 1922–1929
Albatros, Croft Road, 1923–1924
Coventry Victor, Cox Street, 1926–1938/49

Raglan, the well-known cycle company based in Raglan Street, built a prototype car in 1899. It was very similar to the contempory Benz, but unfortunately never made it into production.

Built by Henry Cave, the **Lady** voiturette was powered by a 2¼-h.p. De Dion engine. Drive was via a 'Stow' flexible propshaft to the rear axle, and the body usually fitted was that of a small two-seater. The weight of the car was just 5½ cwt., but it could not manage more than 16 m.p.h.

The **Endurance** Motor Co. was established in 1898, though its first vehicle didn't appear until the following year. The firm's machines were very closely based on Benz designs, with either a 4½- or or 6-h.p. horizontal single-cylinder engine, and two-speed belt transmissions. One example was entered in the Thousand Miles Trial of 1900, but had to retire with mechanical problems.

The Lady was one of the first cars to employ a flexible drive-shaft. Other novel features included a movable steering-column to allow easy access to the seats.

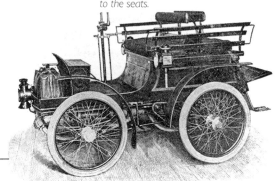

An 1899 Endurance Wagonette with carriage-work by Mulliner of London

The **Billings** was produced by E.D. Billings at the turn of the century. It was sometimes known as the Burns, as it was sold through J. Burns of London. (Burns was also, it is interesting to note, the appointed London agent for Endurance cars.) The Billings, a light, open two-seater voiturette, had a 2¼-h.p. De Dion engine mounted at the front of the car, with a shaft drive and tiller steering. No bonnet was used, and thus the engine was always exposed to the elements.

The 1900 Centaur Autocar

When the **Centaur** Cycle Co. decided to branch into the motor trade in 1900, they did so with a four-seater *dos-à-dos* dogcart. Its 4½-h.p. single-cylinder engine was mounted at

the front, power transmission being via a complicated system of fast-and-loose pulleys, similar to the design employed by Benz. Dunlop pneumatic tyres were fitted to the cycle-built wheels, and the vehicle sold for £220. Centaur didn't build only cars, though. High-quality bicycles, motorcycles and tricars were made at the West Orchard-based factory.

Based in Crow Lane, **Whitley** were suppliers of proprietary engines, though they did build their own 2¾–3¼ h.p.-motorcycles, as well as several different Whitley fore-cars based on their two-wheeled machines. There are no records to show that Whitley built any true cars, although their power units were definitely used by quite a few car producers.

The first **Ryleys** were motorized tricycles and quadricycles, but Messrs Ryley, Ward and Bradford had been developing their tubular-framed light voiturette for nearly two years before they finally put it on the market, in September 1901. It was powered by a single-cylinder MMC engine, rated at 2¾ h.p. A two-speed gearbox was used, with a shaft transmitting the final drive. In the following year, the company built a larger car, incorporating a 5-h.p. Aster engine and three speeds. Unfortunately, car manufacture was to come to an early halt in the same year, leaving J.A. Ryley to face all the debts.

The **Ridley** was a very light two-seater that employed either a 3½-h.p. De Dion or 5-h.p. Buchet power unit. Built by John Ridley, who also designed the machine, it had an

C. Borthwick and John Ridley seated in a 1902 Ridley 3½-h.p. voiturette

ingenious combined gearbox and back axle. These vehicles were produced between 1901 and 1904.

After the failure of the Upper Well Street company, which by now was known as the Ridley Autocar Co. Ltd, semi-finished chassis were ordered from a firm called Horsfall & Bickham, makers of the Horbick, to which Ridley added his own single-cylinder engine. This work was carried out at his private address in Paisley, Renfrewshire, however. A new company was formed in Scotland in 1906, but few cars were ever sold.

Forman were a well-known engine-building firm, their products being supplied to a large number of car manufacturers. Between 1904 and 1906 they built a few vehicles of their own, usually employing Forman 12/14-h.p. two-cylinder or 14-h.p. four-cylinder power units.

The **Aurora** Motor Manufacturing Co. used to advertise themselves as 'motor manufacturers', although there are no records to suggest that they were even engine-builders, let alone car producers. In fact, Aurora used others' proprietary engines to power their limited production motorcycles.

At the 1903 Stanley Automobile Show, the **Hamilton** Motor Co. Ltd showed several motor bikes, a trailer and a fore-car. Hamilton employed engines of their own design, and within the year were also supplying other car manufacturers with their advanced power units. Eventually, Hamilton would concentrate solely on producing proprietary engines for the trade.

Hobart, Bird & Co. entered the car industry with a typical tricar-based trade carrier. Powered by a White & Poppe 4½-h.p. water-cooled engine, with a chain drive to the single rear wheel, their machine was built for a number of years, before production was devoted to motorcycles, the company's original trade.

The **Iden** marque was formed by the ex-MMC works manager, George Iden. The Fleet Street-based firm built two types of four-cylinder cars during 1904: a 12-h.p. and an 18-h.p. model. Both had shaft drives, and were very conventional in appearance for the time.

For 1905, a 25-h.p. car was introduced to complement the two smaller models, but it was to remain in production for only the one season. Towards the end of 1907, Iden built a front-wheel-drive car. It had a 12-h.p. V-twin engine mounted under the front seat, and drive was through a three-speed gearbox. Landaulet bodies were usually fitted, as this vehicle was intended for taxi-cab work as much as private use. Few of these were ever built, and unfortunately, the last Iden cars were produced in the same year.

Richard Henry Lea and Graham Inglesby Francis entered into partnership towards the end of 1895, with the intention of building bicycles. They first moved into Lower Ford Street in the spring of 1896 (the works were the property of Lord Leigh), and production of the cycles got under way shortly afterwards. All the bicycles that the company built were of top quality, and thus rather expensive, many of the

A 1905 12-h.p. Iden

The first Lea-Francis (c. 1903)

components being manufactured in house. Demand began to slacken off after an initial boom, and the last of the bicycles was built during the First World War. Fortunately, **Lea & Francis** had the foresight to predict the decline of the cycle industry before it was too late, and branched out into motor cars around 1903.

Alexander Craig, an independent consulting engineer, was called in to mastermind the project. He had already gained a good reputation through other Coventry firms, such as Maudslay and Standard. His first design for Lea and Francis was rather unconventional, and so to protect the then flourishing cycle business, a new company was formed, called the Lea & Francis Motor Syndicate Ltd. This happened towards the end of June 1903, and it was agreed that two cars had to built within twelve months to a satisfactory standard, or the idea would be shelved.

The task was completed in plenty of time, and a car appeared in chassis form at Crystal Palace early in 1904. Three cars were in fact built by the following year, and one of these was sold to a Mr Hans Renold, the famous chain-manufacturer. Production was temporarily suspended, though, in a bid to collect as much raw material as was financially possible.

In May 1908 it was decided to dispose of the Motor Syndicate, and this was carried through just over a year later; several thousand pounds had been lost on the venture. By 1911, Lea-Francis had joined the growing ranks of motor-cycle manufacturers, and their bikes brought them numerous successes in sporting events, as well as being excellent road machines.

D-type Lea-Francis fixed-head coupé

A few months after the Great War ended and peace was declared, work got under way on a new medium-sized motor car. Several different prototypes of various designs were built, but only a handful were ever sold. The financial position of the company was becoming a serious problem, and early in 1922, an alliance was formed with the Vulcan Motor Engineering Co. of Southport. A new board was selected towards the end of the year.

After previous poor results in the motor trade and the failure of their latest attempt, it was a wonder that the company persisted, though the appointment of the experienced Charles Van Eugen proved to be a turning-point in this epoch of Lea-Francis history. The C-type light car was his first contribution, and this employed an engine designed and built by Meadows in Wolverhampton. The first one was produced in March 1923, and just a few months later the D-type made its debut. Both were very small, but were offered with a variety of body options.

The ponderous Lea-Francis E-type announced towards the end of 1924 certainly bore no resemblance to its Jaguar namesake. Other vehicles with either modified or different engines or gearboxes followed, respectively designated F, I and H. A cheaper model, type G, would also be introduced, but very few were ever built.

Competition successes for the new vehicles were indeed plentiful, mainly in the trials field. Further modifications to the range necessitated new type-letters, and by the start of 1926,

1926 Lea-Francis 12/40 'M'-type

the letter N had been reached, type M being a Super Sports 12/40 chassis.

A totally new model appeared later on in the year; it was marketed as the 14/40. It was also in this year that Lea-Francis made the decision to enter a proper racing programme. As was the case with many works teams, lessons were learnt, and improvements were carried over to the production vehicles. The services of Ron 'Soapy' Sutton would be called upon as the works team number one driver, though he would eventually become famous for his exploits with Alvis, and more particularly Jaguar.

A short time later, a larger six-cylinder machine was introduced: the 16/60. Although it was a vast improvement over the previous model, finances ruled out its good potential ever being developed properly.

The familiar alphabetical designations had by 1928 reached the letter U, but it was the supercharged S-type that is probably best remembered from this last batch of designs. The S-type, or 'Hyper', as it became known, was a direct development from the racing programme, and could be bodied as either an open four-seater, or later as a sports saloon.

The many sporting events entered by the Lea-Francis company saw a fairly good rate of success, but by the end of the year, when the financial results were released, a loss of over £17000 was shown. At about the same time, an interesting project was undertaken: the conversion of a 14/40 to a rotary-valve engine. The project was abandoned, however.

Kaye Don winning the 1928 Tourist Trophy Race in a 1½-litre Lea-Francis Hyper Sports

The V-type was introduced for 1929. It was basically an S-type without the supercharger, but was certainly a very pleasing vehicle none the less.

Lea-Francis became independent again, though almost immediately talks started up for a proposed merger between the Coventry company and Bentley. Eventually, somewhat reluctantly, negotiations broke down.

With increasing financial difficulties (blamed on the Vulcan 14/40 engine), the Francis saloon was introduced, to try to compete with local offerings, but it was the Ace of Spades that would capture the limelight (the name originated from the shape of the engine when viewed from the front). This car was officially launched in September 1930.

Just six months later, however, the receiver was called in. As one would expect, progress slowed down on all fronts, although one 18-h.p. car was built from scratch with a view to production. The receiver naturally rejected the idea, good though it was.

Van Eugen went to Riley in 1934 to help with the new Autovia project, but the following few months saw some hectic activity, and funnily enough several ex-Riley men got together to build a 'Riley-type Lea-Francis'. They had originally traded as Leaf Engineering, and when this company was wound up, they were situated in Holbrooks Lane, having been told to leave the Lower Ford Street factory by the Lea and Francis receiver.

A new company was formed in July 1937: Lea-Francis (1937) Ltd. Premises were obtained in Much Park Street, and then in the old Standard works on the opposite side of the road. Charlesworth Bodies had also been based there, and they were later taken over by the new company.

The first cars were described as 12/50 and 14-h.p. models, available with either six- or four-light bodies. Other, sportier bodies were of course easy to come by, though, with the profusion of local coach-builders. Some would later be listed as additional standard models.

During the Second World War, Lea-Francis would carry out subcontract work for the Ministry of War. Their factory, incidentally, was one of the very fortunate few that were not destroyed during the Blitz. If it had, that would almost certainly have been the end of the company, as they could never have afforded the expense of rebuilding it.

A modified pre-war design was used for the company's first post-war vehicle, but around a year after the hostilities ceased, development started on a 2½-litre engine, shortly to be followed by an independent front suspension system. The first really new car was a six-light saloon, known as the 14/70. Lea-Francis took over Charlesworth for the manufacture of this body, and production got under way in 1948.

Rather surprisingly, the tax-avoiding estate cars and vans still took the highest percentage of sales, despite a particularly nice four-light saloon, and a still-strong racing team. Competition engines were also sold to such famous racing marques as Connaught and HRG.

Sales gradually decreased, owing to stiffer competition from other local companies – Jaguar in particular – and so the final run of cars was cleared from the factory during August 1954. Ministry work kept the company afloat for several more years, but with the loss of this contract, the financial results of 1959 spelt doom for the ailing company. The 1960 Lynx, a pretty roadster, was the last-ditch attempt at survival, but the financial burden proved too great, and the receiver was called in.

The company's assets were finally purchased by Quinton Hazel, the well-known motor spares manufacturer, in late 1962, but only after an unsuccessful attempt to lift Lea-Francis with a final design. Later, A.B. Price of Studley would buy the Lea-Francis name, and he has not only built up a spares and service organization around it, but has also revived the marque. At the 1988 Motor Show, Studley showed the world the new Lea-Francis Ace of Spades saloon, built in limited numbers using modern Jaguar components.

The **Climax** was an assembled car that employed either Aster or White & Poppe engines, three-speed gearboxes and a shaft drive. The George Street-based company initially offered a 10/12-h.p. Aster twin-, a 15-h.p. White & Poppe three-cylinder and 16- and 20-h.p. Aster four-cylinder chassis. These early cars had Rolls-Royce style radiators, but a flat-top was used not long afterwards. For the following year (1906), only four-cylinder models were available: the 14-h.p. White & Poppe and 22-h.p. Aster. A 20-h.p. 'six' was built in 1907, but the company was to cease trading before it could be developed.

A 1949 14/70 Lea-Francis with coachwork by Westland of Hereford. This is the only 14-h.p. car ever to carry this body design.

The Lea-Francis Lynx

A splendid 1906 Climax 20/22

Dalton & Wade often traded under the marque names DAW and D & W. They once built their own motorcycle engines, which were based on a Minerva design, but no further information about the company exists.

The earliest **Hubbards** were all tricars with handlebar steering. They were usually powered by an inclined 4-h.p. single-cylinder water-cooled engine. The next car the company announced was a shaft-driven four-cylinder version with an engine rated at 16/20 h.p. This model stayed in production from 1905 to the firm's departure from the trade in 1910.

Doherty Motor Components Ltd were listed at one time as motor manufacturers, although the only records available – for instance, the 1905 Motor Show catalogue – suggest that they were only parts suppliers.

Arno started building cars in Gosford Street around 1908, having earlier produced several motorcycles. Their first car was displayed at the 1908 Stanley Show, and featured a 20–25 h.p. White & Poppe engine with drive being taken by a universal-jointed propeller shaft to the rear axle. Comment was passed on the vehicle's low price – just £375 – but, even so, the Arno was another of those short-lived makes, and very few were ever sold. Another source suggests that a four-cylinder 35-h.p. engine option was also available, though whether any were built using this unit is not known for sure.

The **Titan** Motor Wheel Co. produced a cheap three-wheeled vehicle between 1911 and 1912. It was powered by a single-cylinder water-cooled engine of Fafnir origin, and this was linked to a two-speed epicyclic gearbox, the whole lot being mounted on an ash frame. Final drive was via a single chain running to the rear wheel. Catalogues suggest its price was around £78.

The 20–25-h.p. Arno, as seen at the 1908 Stanley Show

The **Glover** was an ultra-light cyclecar built by the Glover brothers (Hubert and Harry) of Spon Street. They were originally chemists, and then manufacturers of electrical, mechanical and photographic apparatus, before turning to car-building. The Glover used a 4¼-h.p. single-cylinder Precision engine mounted on a wooden frame, with final drive via belts. The business later moved to Windsor Street, and a total of twelve vehicles were built: a prototype, one for each of the two brothers, and nine for customers.

There were enquiries for the Glover from places as far afield as Australia, South Africa, Nova Scotia, New Zealand, Japan and Bombay – indeed, had the war not intervened, the Glover would have been a great success.

When the brothers were forced to move in 1968, they bought the Biggin Hall Garage on the Binley Road. Hubert's son, Arthur, ran the business until as recently as 1982, but then the garage was sold to somebody outside the family.

Preliminary Leaflet.

GLOVER BROS.
LIGHT TWO-SEATER

(LICENCE — £2 2s.)

Raison d'etre. Many Motorists, whilst objecting to the complication and expensive upkeep of a car, yet require something more sociable than a motor bicycle; at the same time taking exception to a cycle and side-car, as "unmechanical" and "dirty to handle," etc.

We claim that this little machine meets those requirements exactly; being as easily handled as, and more comfortable than a cycle, is light and as clean to use as a car, and is the essence of simplicity.

SPECIFICATION.

Engine —4½ h.p. Air cooled "Precision," specially built specially for us by Messrs. Baker & Co.

Ignition.—H.T. Magneto, controlled from steering wheel.

Chassis.—Ash, of ample strength and elasticity, combining the maximum of safety and comfort, and dispensing with expensive and heavy steel springs.

Wheels.—Cycle Type, 26 in. by 2¼ in.

Tyres.—Dunlop (or other makes by arrangement.)

Brakes.—Rim brakes to back wheels, applied by pedal—to countershaft by hand lever.

Transmission.—From engine to countershaft by 3 in. flat belt; from countershaft to back wheels by 1 in. V belt.

Speeds.—Two, operated by side lever, free engine by pedal.

Body.—Upholstered in "Pegamoid," woodwork painted to suit customer.

Carburettor.—Amac, controlled from steering wheel.

Steering.—15 in. Wheel, "Exonite" covered.

MANUFACTURERS:

GLOVER BROS.
Windsor Street, COVENTRY.

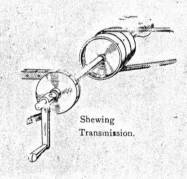

Shewing Transmission.

The manufacturers reserve the right to make such alterations and improvements as may be deemed advisable, from time to time, without notice.

'Preliminary leaflet' released by the Glover brothers, showing the prototype Glover light car

An early Crouch Carette

Work devoted to the war effort took up the next few years, but soon afterwards the firm was employing around 400 men and producing between twenty and thirty cars a week. The first bodies came from Carbodies on the Holyhead Road, but an old munitions factory was purchased, enabling Crouch to carry out their own coach-building operations.

By 1922, Crouch had built a replacement model. The engine (still a V-twin), was now mounted at the front of the car, and a shaft drive was employed to transmit the power. These new twins ran in both the 1922 and the 1923 200 Mile Race at Brooklands. The marque soon gained a sporting reputation, and one racing driver in particular helped to establish this: Stirling Moss's father, Alfred. As well as racing, Alfred Moss handled the London sales.

A new Anzani-powered four-cylinder model was added to the range in 1923, and this could be bought with a 'Super Sports' specification. Ninety m.p.h. was its reputed top speed, but this made the vehicle very expensive.

A serious blow came when 200 cars ordered from Australia were despatched and none of them was paid for. The business came to an unfortunate end in 1927, but the company which had first been based in Bishop Street, then Cook Street, and then had body-building premises on the Stoney Stanton Road as well, had come a long way. Later Crouch models, usually small four-cylinder light cars, had lost

The marque name of **Crouch** came into being when John W.F. Crouch and his father, also called John, formed Crouch Motors (1910) Ltd. The first Crouch was originally a three-wheeled cyclecar, known as the Carette. From 1913, it became available as a four-wheeler, and was powered by a 1-litre Coventry Simplex engine. This water-cooled V-twin was centrally mounted, and this gave the car a snub-nosed appearance. Three forward gears and a chain drive were used.

Ian Parker driving a sporting Crouch, 1923

all resemblance to their humble cyclecar beginnings. It is interesting to note that Crouch Cars Ltd, even as one of the more successful smaller manufacturers, managed to build only around 3000 cars in their entire lifetime.

When George Woodcock gained control of the Wolverhampton-based cycle firm of Daniel Rudge in 1880, he proceeded to merge this with his other business: the Coventry Cycle Co. Five years later, financial assistance led to the creation of Daniel Rudge & Co., which, following another amalgamation in 1893, became known as Rudge-Whitworth & Co. Ltd.

The small **Rudge** cyclecar was built at the Rudge-Whitworth works in Crow Lane, Coventry, and shared many features with the Rudge-Multi motorcycle, including a variable gear operated by expanding pulley. A 750-c.c. single-cylinder air-cooled engine powered the machine, with final drive being transmitted through belts. The body was that of a staggered two-seater, and was very low in appearance.

Unfortunately, the vehicle was never to achieve the fame of the Rudge motorcycles, and so it was withdrawn from the market in 1913, less than a year after its introduction. Ironically, it was probably Rudge-Whitworth's success in other areas that stopped the development of car production.

The **Broadway** was a typical cyclecar powered by an air-cooled Fafnir engine of 8 h.p. V-belts were used for the final drive, and the machine sold for only £80. It was listed on the market for just one year – 1913.

Powered by a two-cylinder engine of the company's own manufacture, the **Taylor-Swetnam** was a light car which carried a two-seater streamlined body. Drive was via a three-speed gearbox and a shaft, and the vehicle usually sold for around £140. A larger car with a French-built four-cylinder engine was said to be in preparation for 1914, but nothing appeared, and the firm ceased trading in 1913 – the year in which it had started.

The **Williamson** three-wheeler had an 8-h.p. two-cylinder Douglas engine with a chain drive to the single rear wheel. Fitted with a two-seater body, it was very similar in appearance to contemporary Morgans. The war interrupted all Williamson production, and car-building did not resume when peace returned. However, the firm's motorcycles would remain on the market until around 1920.

The **Alpha** wasn't in fact the name of a car, but an engine. It was built by a company known as Johnson, Hurley & Martin, and was very successful at the time. It seems that production started quite some time before the First World War, with the hostilities interrupting briefly, until full-scale engine-building got under way again shortly afterwards. Several car manufacturers employed Alpha engines, one such company being Calthorpe. Fitted with Alpha engines, Calthorpes gained fourth place overall in the 1908 Tourist Trophy Race, and consistently won gold medals in the Irish Reliability Trials. Four-cylinder engines were an Alpha speciality, though in the early days two-cylinder versions were also listed.

The **Dawson** was designed by the former works manager of Hillman's, A.J. Dawson. It was a high-quality light car, being manufactured rather than assembled, and used an advanced

1920 Dawson car

1795-c.c., 11.9-h.p. four-cylinder single o.h.c. engine. Bodies were by Charlesworth, and could be either open or closed. Cross & Ellis built a smart coupé body on the Dawson chassis in 1920, but the high prices of Dawson cars (between £750 and £995) meant that very few were ever sold – about sixty-five are thought to have been produced – and Triumph acquired the factory for their new car in 1921.

The **Barnett** company was once listed as a motor manufacturer, but unfortunately no records exist to confirm this. It is more likely that they simply built engines.

Clarke, Cluley & Co. was founded as a textile-machine producer in the Globe Works, Well Street, in 1890. The firm didn't start building cars until 1922, although they had earlier built bicycles, as well as a tricar called the Globe Cymocar in 1904.

The **Cluley**, in its most famous form, was a typical light car of the early twenties, with proprietary four-cylinder engines of either 10 or 11.9-h.p. A six-cylinder model was announced for 1924, with a four-cylinder o.h.v. 14/50-h.p. vehicle being introduced four years later. However, few, if any, of these last two Cluleys were ever built. Car production ceased in 1929, and the company turned its efforts back towards the textile-machinery industry at its newer factory, situated in Kenilworth. During the early part of 1988, Clarke, Cluley & Co. moved to their new factory near Baginton airport, where most of their work is now for the Westland helicopter company.

The **Albatros** was built by Albert Ross in Croft Road between 1923 and 1924. It was a very conventional light car, and was fairly typical of type, with no two vehicles alike. Either 8- or 10-h.p. Coventry Climax engines were used, with a differential being fitted to the 10-h.p. model. Usually the chassis was fitted with either a two- or a four-seater open body, and whilst some had artillery wheels, others had the disc type. Production figures differ wildly, depending on which source one believes, between 40 and 180, but it is more likely that the smaller figure is correct. Only one 10-h.p. and one 8-h.p. vehicle are thought to survive.

The Cox Street-based company of **Coventry Victor** were more famous during the early years for their small proprietary engines, though they did build a three-wheeled cyclecar for a while as well. Oddly, it was produced when only Morgan persisted with that design, the light car having driven the type virtually out of existence.

A prototype four-wheeled light car was built in 1919.

Cluley car production may have been as high as 3000 units, but today a Cluley is a very rare find.

The Albatros – a rare bird!

Designed by W.A. Weaver, the company's managing director, it employed the same engine as was used on the new Coventry Victor motorcycles, but the vehicle was never put into production. Not until 1926 did another car appear.

The Coventry Victor Family model was powered by a water-cooled side-valve flat-twin engine of 688 c.c. This, with the engine enlarged to 749 c.c., was used for competition purposes, and marketed as the 'Sport'. Chains were used to transmit the final drive, and no self-starter was included. Not until 1932 did a starter become available, and this Beauvais-styled 'Luxury Sports' version continued in production through to 1937, by which time 850-, 900- and 1000-c.c. engines had been used.

In 1949 the company built several small saloon prototypes using light flat-four engines. Code-named 'Venus', unfortunately the vehicles never made it into production, and these were to be the last ever made by the factory. However, the company continued to build various engines, and still do to this day, though they now trade as A.N. Weaver (Coventry Victor) Ltd, close to the old Humber works.

A Coventry Victor three-wheeler, shown in the firm's workshops in the 1950s

4

THE NORTHERNERS

THE INDUSTRIAL DEVELOPMENT SITES AT THE NORTHERN END OF THE CITY HAVE PLAYED HOST TO MANY MANUFAC- TURERS OVER THE YEARS. RILEY AND JAGUAR WERE THE MOST FAMOUS. HERE WE LOOK AT THE LESS WELL-KNOWN.

Progress, Foleshill Road, 1899–1903
West-Aster, Foleshill Road, 1904–1913
Academy, Foleshill Road, 1906–1908
Also included:
Ranger, West Orchard, 1913–1914

Duryea, Widdrington Road, 1902–1906
Lotis, Widdrington Road, 1908–1912

Payne & Bates, Foleshill Road, 1900–1901
Brooks, Holbrook Lane, 1901–1902
Carlton, Lockhurst Lane, 1901–1902
Lee-Stroyer, East Street, 1903
Forge, Holbrook Lane, 1903–1905
Record, Stoney Stanton Road, 1905
Eagle, Foleshill Road, 1912–1913
Challenge, Foleshill Road, 1912–1915
Remington, Foleshill Road, 1919–1930
Bayliss, Thomas & Co., Stoney Stanton Road, 1920–1927
Cooper, Lythalls Lane, 1922–1923
Awson, Awson Street, 1926–1930

The Progress Voiturette of 1900, its De Dion engine set at the rear

When Enoch J. West left the Calcott brothers, he departed to form Progress Cycles. His first vehicle, the **Progress** voiturette of 1899, was originally powered by either a 3½-h.p. De Dion or 4½-h.p. MMC engine, mounted at the rear. The *vis-à-vis* body could be ordered as a two- or four-seater.

For 1902, a new model was introduced. This had a pressed-steel frame and a front-mounted engine of either Aster or De Dion origins. An 8-h.p. two-cylinder Daimler unit was also available, but in any case, the bodies were always built by Mulliners. By the end of 1903, the Progress business had gone into liquidation, but an Aster-engined model reappeared during the following year; although basically unchanged, it was to be known as the West.

The first few cars used 10/12-h.p. Aster engines, although some of the earlier examples carried White & Poppe units. When West Ltd. was founded in 1906, the Aster engine was standardized, and thus the cars became generally known as **West-Asters.** It was also around this time that West started building **Academy** cars for the Motor Academy in Notting Hill Gate, London. These vehicles were produced between 1906 and 1908, and were fitted with duplicate clutch and brake controls. Apart from this novel feature, the design followed the usual West practice, although White & Poppe engines of 14/20-h.p. rating were employed. One example was entered in the 1906 Tourist Trophy Race, but unfortunately had to retire after just three laps.

By 1908, a whole range of two- and four-cylinder West-Aster cars, from 10/12- to 35-h.p., were on the market, as well as a line of delivery vans and taxis. A West-Aster taxi was the first British car of its type to pass the Scotland Yard test for use in London. However, by May 1908, the company was in the hands of the receiver, and production ceased.

The story doesn't end here, though, as the original company of E.J. West continued in business as a maker of chassis for other firms, including Singer, Heron, Scout and Pilot. The odd few cars were assembled during 1909, using White & Poppe 16-h.p. engines, and in 1911, a friction-drive light car was announced. It was to be powered by a single-cylinder West engine of 7/9-h.p. rating, but the model never made it into production.

An impressive West-Aster (1908)

In 1913, a new factory was acquired to produce the West cyclecar. This made use of the two-cylinder Chater-Lea engine, although once full production began in the following year, a Precision power unit was employed, and the marque name of **Ranger** was adopted. 1914 models retained two-speed gearboxes and a chain final drive, but either Alpha or Blumfield engines replaced the original unit. The last Ranger was built towards the end of 1914.

Enoch West wasn't the only industrialist based in the north – Henry Sturmey of *Autocar* also ran one of his business interests in the area, that of **Duryea**. This American firm represented the commercial endeavours of Charles E. Duryea, who, with his brother Frank, built one of America's first cars. This happened around 1892, and the company progressed steadily in the following years. Two examples brought over from the States took an active part in the famous Emancipation Run from London to Brighton in 1896.

Sturmey had originally wanted to build the world's first £100 motor car, which in those early days would have been a unique achievement. One vehicle was built using an MMC 2¾-h.p. engine and a basketwork body. Having given up with this first idea, Sturmey formed the British Duryea Co.

Between 1902 and 1906, three- and four-wheeled vehicles, powered by rear-mounted transverse three-cylinder engines were built under licence in Coventry. They featured two-speed crypto gears and tiller steering. The tiller also housed the gear selector and throttle, thus giving the car a single lever control. At the beginning of 1902, a Duryea could be purchased in England for around £275. These Coventry-built models were powered by engines from

The DURYEA

POWER SURREY or Double Phaeton.

This elegant carriage is especially designed for comfort. The passengers in the rear seat are elevated above those in front. There is room for two children on the seat in front in addition to the four regular seats of the vehicle.

PRINCIPAL FEATURES.—Three cylinder balanced engine. Single chain (noiseless) transmission. Absence of noisy wasteful gearing. No bevel gears. No pumps. One-piece live axle. Simplicity throughout. 10 h.p. Weight 900 lbs., and

ONE HAND DOES IT ALL.

Write for illustrated catalogue of our unique cars—
THE DURYEA CO., COVENTRY.

N.B.—Trials can be arranged in Coventry by appointment.

An advertisement from 1902 for Duryea

Williams & Robinson, but unfortunately, the British Duryea faded away in 1906, and the factory was then used to build the **Lotis** car.

The Sturmey Motor Co. was formed after British Duryea disappeared, and was floated in January 1907. It wasn't until the following year, though, that the first Lotis car left the Widdrington Road factory. The original Lotis models had either a 10/12- or 12/18-h.p. two-cylinder engine mounted underneath the seat. From 1909, these Riley-manufactured units were moved forward and placed under a coal-scuttle bonnet, an arrangement typical of the time.

In 1910 a new range of cars which used White & Poppe engines of either 16/20-, 20/25- or 25/35-h.p. rating were introduced. A light car known as the Lotis-Parsons was also being built as a 'colonial pleasure car', but the idea came too late, and production ceased altogether during 1912.

The partnership of **Payne & Bates** was formed in 1897. They designed and built their own engines, and then progressed to producing cars. Walter Payne established himself in Godiva Street during 1890, where he built small stationary gas engines. He was reputed to have built, in the mid-1890s, the first petrol engine in Coventry, and was obviously a very fine engineer. An injection of cash from his wife's uncle, George Bates, allowed Payne to develop and diversify.

The earliest cars were almost direct copies of the single-cylinder Benz that Mr Payne had acquired in 1897, as the company were still really gas-engine manufacturers who made a number of experimental vehicles. Payne & Bates were to build the Godiva car between 1900 and 1901, at their factory on the Foleshill Road. Hawkins & Peake looked after the bodywork of the first prototype, but the company eventually had its own body shop.

A small series of vehicles were produced for a company in Lincoln. The car was then marketed as the Stonebow, and featured a 9-h.p. two-cylinder engine, mounted up front. It had a double chain drive, and carried a four-seater *dos-à-dos* body. Other outlets into the horseless-carriage field included Pat Hamilton of Coventry, for whom Payne & Bates built two cars known simply as Shamrocks. The International Motor Car Co. of London also asked Payne & Bates (and Allard of Coventry), to design new cars for them, but no real success came of the project.

During 1901, the company advertised 7-, 9-, 14- and 25-h.p. models, with either two- or four-cylinder engines. By now, the business had its own foundry, smithy, machine-shop, test-shop, drawing office, and bodywork and paint-shop, but the end was to come in March 1902. George Bates was fatally injured whilst out driving on one of his cars, and so the Payne family decided to wind up the company. The Foleshill Road factory was sold to the makers of Radenite batteries, and the small workshop in Castle Street was reopened. Here Walter Payne continued to produce car and other engines until his death in 1934. Just one Stonebow and one Godiva are the sole survivors of the marque, the latter being kept in Coventry's Museum of British Road Transport.

The **Brooks** was a short-lived light car built by Mr H. Brooks in Holbrook Lane. It used Pinart engines supplied by Van Raden's of either 8- or 12-h.p. rating, mounted at the

Lotis 12/18 (c. 1909)

The sole surviving Payne & Bates Godiva (1901)

1902 Brooks. Note the radiator at the front of the car, under the bonnet.

Ted Hewitt admiring one of the Climax FWA racing engines which he helped to test and develop. This one is fitted in a Lotus XI, and is an o.h.c. unit of 1097 c.c.

Coventry Climax engines powered many Grand Prix cars. This one is a 1966 Lotus 33.

front, with drive being transmitted by a shaft. The customer had the choice of either two- or four-seater coachwork.

In the short space of time in which **Carlton** built cars, three models were listed. All of them made use of Aster engines, and the range consisted of a 6-h.p. single-cylinder, a 12-h.p. twin-, and a 24-h.p. four-cylinder chassis. When car production came to an end in 1902, the company manufactured various small motors, parts and accessories for the trade, including a 5-h.p. vertical engine along De Dion lines.

Both the **Forge** Motor Syndicate Ltd and the **Record** Motor Co. were listed as motor manufacturers, but no records exist to say what their trades actually were. **Eagle** were also listed as motor manufacturers, although the only record of the company suggests its trade was that of electrical-component suppliers to the motor industry. **Challenge** used to advertise themselves as car and motorcycle producers, but there is nothing to suggest that any of either were built under the Challenge marque name. The **Remington** Motor Co. is another mysterious business – engines seem to have been the firm's only product associated with the car trade.

Although very little is known about the **Lee-Stroyer**, its background is a very interesting one. Its origins go back to the start of the century, when a certain H. Pelham Lee returned from the Boer War and set up a small engineering business in East Street, Coventry.

Although Lee began his engineering career on the electrical side of the trade, he soon felt that his future lay with the internal-combustion engine. After completing his military service, he finished his training with Daimler before founding the East Street firm in 1903. A partnership was formed between Lee and a Dane named Stroyer.

It is thought that the Lee-Stroyer car was built partly to demonstrate the efficiency of Lee's petrol engine, and partly for Lee's pleasure. It was decided, however, at quite an early stage that the idea of producing complete cars would have to be abandoned, to avoid tying up the firm's limited capital for long periods of time. To concentrate on engine-building was the only answer, so when Stroyer left the company in 1905, new premises were acquired (part of the old Gosford Green Humber works), and Coventry Simplex engines came into being.

Coventry Simplex engines were used by many motor manufacturers over the following years, and a certain amount of work was carried out for the War Office during the First World War. It was during this period that the Coventy Climax name was adopted. The production of motor-car engines had taken up most of the Coventry Climax capacity from around 1920 to 1936, but in the following year, a new and lucrative market opened up for the company: fire pumps. The Climax engines were adapted for all kinds of uses during the Second World War, and the works could hardly keep up with demand.

Shortly after the war, Climax once again branched out into a totally new venture. This time it was fork-lift trucks. The first model, the ET199, was built just before the end of 1946, and served as a good prototype on which to build. The need for a new, lighter and more powerful fire pump led to the introduction of the FW, but an unlikely turn of events saw

1925 11.9-h.p. Bayliss, Thomas

the engine develop over the ensuing years into a highly successful racing engine. It went on to power several sports cars and even Formula One Grand Prix cars. Coventry Climax became part of the Jaguar group of companies in March 1963, but continued with most of their projects unchanged. After regaining independence during the early eighties, Kalmar Industries purchased the business in December 1986, and promptly renamed the company Kalmar-Climax.

Kalmar have branches all over the world, but in the United Kingdom they produce a wide variety of lifting equipment. In more recent years, the business has been known simply as Kalmar U.K., though it is still rightfully very proud of its heritage in Coventry.

Bayliss, Thomas & Co. were one of the few Coventry firms to produce 2000 bicycles in a year. It took other companies several years to catch up with this impressive output figure. By the turn of the century, however, the business was recording serious trading deficits. The partnership of Bayliss and Thomas began in 1874, when they founded their company and started to manufacture the Excelsior bicycle. Motorcycles followed in 1896, but it would be many years before automobiles were attempted.

Towards the end of 1919, Bayliss, Thomas & Co. experimented with an air-cooled three-wheeler which featured an independent front suspension. This led to the Excelsior four-wheeler of 1921, but by now, the business had been taken over by R. Walker & Sons, the Birmingham-based lamp-makers.

All production was transferred to Tyseley, and the Coventry factory became the home of Francis-Barnett motorcycles. None the less, not all links with the city were immediately lost, as Coventry Simplex engines powered several Birmingham-built models, before eventually being replaced by Meadows units.

The original **Cooper** car was built in Bedford. It used a vertical three-cylinder air-cooled engine, but only the one prototype was ever built. When the company moved to Lythalls Lane in Coventry, Cooper produced several conventional light cars, employing Coventry Climax engines and Moss gearboxes. They had long, rakish bonnets, and the radiators were of German silver. Cooper also made the 1½-litre Janvier-engined Warwick racing car which entered for the 1923 200 Mile Race at Brooklands.

The **Awson** Motor Carriage Co. Ltd are mentioned in the Register of Business Records of Coventry and related areas, but it merely states that all of the firm's records were destroyed. The Coventry directories from the time show Awson were heavily involved in accessories, so this may have been their only trade.

5

MARQUES FROM THE EAST

A HISTORY OF THE COMPANIES, SOME PAST AND SOME PRESENT, TO THE EASTERN SIDE OF THE CITY.

Swift, Cheylesmore, 1899–1931
Coronet, Far Gosford Street, 1903–1906
Marseal, Harefield Road, 1919–1925
Emms, Walsgrave Road, 1922–1923
Ariel, Ordnance Works, 1922–1925
Wigan-Barlow, Lowther Street, 1922–1923
Omega, Swan Lane, 1925–1927
Warwick, Walsgrave Road, 1926–1930
Ferguson, Baginton, 1952–
Andy Rouse Engineering, Progress Way, 1983–

As mentioned in the first chapter of this book, the Swift Cycle Co. was formed in 1896, from a firm originally involved in the textile industry. It wasn't until Josiah Turner was persuaded to build a run of 400 cycles during the 1860s that Swift became a marque name. The company could rightfully claim to be the oldest British cycle-manufacturer, as their first machine appeared nearly a year before the debut of the Humber cycle. The old works manager, James Starley, with his many friends and relatives from the Swift company, went on to found several other Coventry firms, including Rover, Hillman, Singer, Humber, Ariel and Rudge, to mention but a few.

Swift were one of the many companies that progressed from building bicycles to motorcycles and quads, before finally deciding to go in for car production. The first motor-powered Swift was a tricycle, based very closely on an Ariel design, and this was produced in 1898. Ariel-style motor-cycles continued to be built until 1915.

Their first car, built towards the end of 1899, was a small voiturette, with a tubular chassis and a single-cylinder engine from MMC. The Swift Motor Co. was formed in 1902, and was based in Cheylesmore. This left the cycle side of the business to concentrate on their own machines, although they did build several hundred cyclecars during 1912 and 1913.

A more conventional 5½-h.p. car was introduced in 1902, and initially Swifts built their own type of transmission, though this proved to be unreliable, and was changed in 1903 in favour of a more orthodox system. By now several makers' engines had appeared in Swifts, but it wasn't until 1904 that a new model was offered, and this was about the time when the superb Swift-built twin-cylinder 9/10-h.p. engine was added as an extra power unit. Later, it would be used in three-cylinder form; it stayed in production for a number of years.

Swift concentrated on small, light cars, and soon built up a good reputation for reliability and economy, emphasized by a class win in the 1903 Thousand Miles Reliability Trials. By now, because of the demand for Swift products, the company found itself short of space. Thus, new premises were bought in Quinton Road, leaving the old Cheylesmore site to the bicycle side of the business.

The new models quickly led to bigger versions being made available; both a three- and four-cylinder machine were to be offered, but in 1909, another single-cylinder car of 7-h.p. rating made its debut. This vehicle, incidentally, was also sold by Austin, although its life with Swift was a short one, most sales still coming from a two-cylinder light car. This particular model was replaced in 1912 by a new 7-h.p. cyclecar with a shaft drive built by the Swift Cycle Co. This cyclecar was noted for its success in the reliability trials, and other competitions, of the time.

By now, Swift's were one of the major volume manufacturers in the city, placed high in the list with the likes of Humber, Rover and Singer. For 1914, the Swift Motor Co. offered a light car that was basically a cyclecar, but with a pressed-steel chassis in place of the tubular one. From this date, the Swift Cycle Co. would build no more bicycles, and the two firms eventually merged to form Swift of Coventry Ltd during 1919. It was at this time that a Tipton company by the name of Harper Bean acquired 50 per cent of Swift's. When they folded, in the following year, they nearly took Swift's with them.

Swift provided many items to help towards the war effort from around 1916, including several complete aero-engines.

THE HANDIEST—THE LEAST EXPENSIVE TO BUY OR TO RUN—AND THE MOST RELIABLE OF ALL MOTOR CARS IS THE FAMOUS

SWIFT
LIGHT CAR.

PRICE
COMPLETE
WITH ENTIRE
ROAD EQUIPMENT

£140

ALL THE BIG
CAR'S COMFORT,
RELIABILITY,
EFFICIENCY,
AND **NATTINESS**
OF
APPEARANCE.

DO YOU GOLF ? If so, the links are always easily and quickly accessible, this little car can get into many places inaccessible to the big one. Ready at a moment's notice.

FOR THE LADIES. No other car is so particularly suitable to the lady driver; easy of control, light of handling, simple in every aspect, it is the ideal vehicle for the lady motorist.

AS A RUNABOUT it is without an equal, station work, emergency runs to tradesmen, and the other hundred-and-one calls which arise in the daily round, can all be dealt with without delay, fuss, expense, or chauffeur's time.

GENERAL UPKEEP is not nearly so costly as in the case of the big car ; petrol, tyres, etc., go very much further, whilst general maintenance costs are purely nominal.

ALL-ROUND SERVICE. This little car affords big car service and comfort —its mileage and hill-climbing powers have been demonstrated again and again—

THE PRESS, THE TRADE, AND THE PUBLIC have each placed their seal of approval on this, the latest "SWIFT" triumph, and if you will send for a copy of catalogue, complete specification, etc., we will send with them evidence of press, trade, and public appreciation.

THE SWIFT MOTOR CO., LIMITED——COVENTRY.

LONDON :
Holborn Viaduct.

DUBLIN :
South King Street.

An advertisement for a very early Swift

The pretty, if not entirely successful, 1910 7-h.p. Swift

After the war, Swift once again built the 1100-c.c. four-cylinder 'Ten', which had been introduced just before the hostilities began, and a new 2-litre 'Twelve', similar in design to the smaller model. From now on, all Swifts would be four-cylinder cars, regardless of trends. Not noted for their power, the marque's cars were always strong and simple, as well as being the ideal utility vehicle. After the Bean disaster, new management soon got the company back on its feet, and Charles Van Eugen joined the company, maintaining the quality in the marque that William Radford had continued since the firm's beginnings.

Around 1923, the Ten was brought more up to date, with the Twelve receiving the same treatment a little while later, becoming known as the 14/40 h.p. in 1926. It was in the same year that the Ten's engine was enlarged slightly to 1.2 litres. Wire wheels became an option in 1927, and the four-speed gearbox was introduced during 1929. By the following year, the Ten had been given a new narrow radiator shell, and the model was available either with a fabric saloon or tourer body, or with Swallow two-door saloon coachwork. In 1931, this range was augmented by the 8-h.p. Cadet two-door saloon, which, in its cheapest form, cost only £149.

Unfortunately, the company was forced to stop all car production in April of the same year, mainly due to the mass producers, with whom Swift's could not possibly hope to compete. The premises, along with all the tooling, were bought by Alfred Herbert Ltd, Coventry's most famous

10-h.p. Swift (1925)

machine-tool company, with the spares and the Swift name going to different Birmingham concerns. The remaining 8-h.p. engines that were on order from Coventry Climax were built into highly successful Climax FSM fire pumps. To this day, the Swift bicycle continues to be built by a company called Kirk & Merrifield, which at least keeps the name alive.

The **Coronet** Motor Co. was founded in 1903. It was based in Far Gosford Street, and initially started by building motorcycles. The company began to expand slightly, and it was decided to move into car manufacture in 1904.

16-h.p. Coronet (c. 1903)

At first, two models were available: an 8-h.p. single-cylinder and a 16-h.p. four-cylinder. (The latter had the very odd firing order of 1, 2, 3, 4!) The radiator, ignition coil and springs were imported from France, but the rest of the car's components were British made. A 12-h.p. two-cylinder model was added to the range for 1905, and, like its larger 16-h.p. brother, had a shaft drive, and a four-seater tonneau body.

Marseal sports car (1923)

It is interesting to note that Coronet's chief engineer was Walter Iden, the son of George Iden (of MMC fame). Unfortunately, like so many of the early companies, Coronet was destined to be bought out by a larger concern. Early in 1906 Humber acquired the factory.

The marque of **Marseal** was originally known as the Marseel, a combination of the names of the two men who founded the company. In 1919, a Brooklands enthusiast, Captain D.M.K. Marendaz, in partnership with a gentleman by the name of Seelhaft, set about building an orthodox light car, which was to be assembled using fairly standard components. This first vehicle had a 1½ litre, four-cylinder side-valve engine from Coventry Simplex, a three-speed gearbox, and a worm-driven rear axle.

Seelhaft withdrew from the company in 1922, and it was then that the decision was made to name future models Marseal – to make them appear less foreign! A 1¼-litre 11/27-h.p. vehicle was also made. This and the 12/40-h.p. 1½-litre model would become the best-remembered examples to come from the Harefield Road factory. Their rugged and solid chassis, combined with good performance, meant that Marseals did well in trials. Sports versions were built of both cars; the Sport 12/40 was said to be capable of around 75 m.p.h.

The cars were improved in the early part of 1923 and given a power-to-weight ratio approaching that of a racing car – indeed, Marendaz used his cars on several occasions for racing and record-breaking at Brooklands. One or two obscure 1.7-litre six-cylinder models were built, but in 1925

1906 Ariel 35-h.p. tourer driven by Mr P. Lewis, chauffeur and chief tester to Charles Sangster

the Marseal name was dropped and replaced by that of 'Marendaz Special'. The business moved to London shortly afterwards, and was renamed D.M.K. Marendaz Ltd. Here it stayed for a number of years. Another move was made in 1932, this time to Maidenhead. Marendaz's 15/90 model from the mid-1930s was powered by a Coventry Climax engine; it was to be one of his last projects, as he stopped building automobiles in 1937.

Emms began building their light cars on the Walsgrave Road during 1922. They used 9.8-h.p. Coventry Simplex engines coupled to three-speed gearboxes, and a worm drive. Three types of body were available: a two-seater tourer, a closed coupé body and a pointed-tail sports model. Production came to a sudden end in 1923.

The name of **Ariel** is one of the oldest in the industry. Whitehurst & Co. had marketed the Ariel wheel as long ago as 1847, and then James Starley and William Hillman produced their 'ordinary' Ariel bicycles in 1871. The name moved around for a little while, before eventually coming back to Coventry just before the First World War.

The first Ariel car was introduced at the 1901 National Show – a twin-cylinder 10-h.p. machine with a tonneau body. During its turbulent history, Ariel had made arrangements for their cars to be built at the Coventry Ordnance Co., a branch of Cammell Laird. Several models were built until production was turned over completely to war-work and motorcycles in 1916.

During 1915, the car and motorcycle companies were registered as one business, known as The Ariel Works Ltd. After the war, it was motorcycles that became the firm's staple product, although a design was released from the factory which eventually became the Rover 8.

With the small-car boom in full swing, Ariel tried to cash in with a simple three-seater powered by 1-litre air-cooled flat-twin engine named the Ariel Nine. The engine was noisy and suffered from bad vibration, so a new and better unit was employed during the following year. Even so, production was still halted in 1925, and no more cars were to leave the factory. The manufacture of quality motorcycles continued right through to 1970, by which time control of the company had shifted several times.

The **Wigan-Barlow** was a Lowther Street conventionally built assembled car of which very few were ever produced. The 1922 pilot models were made using either a 1368-c.c. Coventry Simplex or a 1496-c.c. Meadows four-cylinder engine. In both cases, a Wrigley back axle was employed. When the car was introduced, it was named the 10-25 h.p., and sold at £450 for the standard two-seater and £505 for the standard four-seater. Alternatively, a chassis only was available at £350. Later in 1922 a sports model made its debut, along with several other versions, but by the following year production had come to an end.

The **Omega** was built by W.J. Green, who had been building motorcycles of the same name for a number of years. The manufacture of the Omega three-wheeler began in 1925. It employed a 980-c.c. JAP engine which drove a single rear wheel via a chain. Several models were available: a standard version, a de luxe model and two 'Family' options priced at between £105 and £125.

The firm of S.H. Newsome was based on the Walsgrave Road. The car they marketed was the **Warwick,** produced by Cooper's of Lythalls Lane, and it was raced by Sam Newsome himself in several sports-car events at Brooklands. Unfortunately, the car was not to prove the great success it was hoped to be. As a garage, S.H. Newsome would go on to be large distributors for many local car manufacturers.

The **Ferguson** marque is one of great importance, but one about which little is recorded. Its story features three men: Major Tony Rolt, Freddie Dixon, the ex-racing driver, and Harry Ferguson, a name synonymous with tractors rather than motor cars. Although there's nothing particularly new about four-wheel drive – the first racing car to be so equipped was the Dutch Spyker, built in 1902 – it is thanks to Ferguson that its development continued, ultimately resulting in modern supercars like the Audi Quattro.

Freddie Dixon had been something of a childhood hero for Rolt, and when he himself started racing, it was Dixon's garage he chose to prepare his car. From this first meeting, the two became friends, and Dixon showed Rolt a model of a Land Speed Record car he had designed. One of the most important features of the vehicle was a radial engine which drove all four wheels. Without financial backing, the project had little future, but it was suggested that a racing car could be built with a similar type of transmission. The engine from Tony Rolt's ERA was promptly put forward for use in a prototype, and in 1939 work began in earnest.

A company was founded in Reigate called Dixon/Rolt Developments, but the Second World War soon intervened, and any ideas of a racing car were put on hold. The

An Omega three-wheeler, with polished aluminium bodywork (1925)

Stirling Moss in the P99 during practice for the 1961 British Grand Prix

next plan of action was to try to sell their four-wheel-drive system to the military, but as no prototype was available for demonstration, little interest was shown. When Tony joined the Army, the ERA was left to gather dust whilst Freddie took on engineering work to help towards the war effort.

After the war, and in between military commitments (he stayed on in the Army), Rolt found enough spare time to help construct a vehicle known as the Crab. Based on a backbone chassis, it was powered by the old Riley 1½-litre engine, and had not only four-wheel drive, but four-wheel steering. In the meantime, Harry Ferguson had moved to England, and began looking up old acquaintances from his earlier days. Ferguson had met Dixon in Ireland when Freddie was racing there in the Tourist Trophy races of the early thirties and, Ferguson being an exceptional engineer with his heart in the car business, they had always had plenty to talk about.

Once Ferguson was told of the Dixon-Rolt partnership and their plans, he offered to help with finances, providing the company developed a four-wheel-drive passenger vehicle rather than a racing car. As the project began to gather momentum, Claude Hill from Aston Martin was called in to provide the necessary technical expertise. In 1950, another company was formed: Harry Ferguson Research Ltd, and the business moved into new premises in Reigate.

Eventually, a completely new rear-engined car known as the R2 was built, the Crab being retrospectively dubbed the R1. Since Ferguson's other main interest, his tractor plant, was based in Coventry, he arranged in the summer of 1952 for the company to move into a small workshop in the Banner Lane factory. However, following the sale of the tractor plant to Massey-Harris, workshops were found at the Chipping Warden aerodrome. Then the company moved back to Coventry again, to a new site at Toll Bar End. By this time, the R3 had been built, and whilst work continued on the Ferguson 2-litre engine, a Jowett unit was fitted to allow testing to continue. The car had many revolutionary features, several being incorporated into its Maxaret anti-skid braking system, developed from those seen on aircraft undercarriages.

The first complete four-wheel-drive prototype was the R4. A four-door body was specially made, with lines similar to those of a Morris Oxford, and test drives were given to the press. Ferguson, meanwhile, was approaching various British car manufacturers, including Len Lord and John Black,

with his ideas. The Alvis management were also contacted, but little came of the discussions that followed.

The team followed in the footsteps of Cisitalia-Porsche and Mercedes-Benz when they took their Grand Prix racing car to the tracks in 1960. Neither of the aforementioned teams had had any real success with their systems, though, and soon went back to a conventional transmission. The Coventry Climax-powered Ferguson also featured Maxaret braking on all-round discs, and a fully independent suspension. Unfortunately, Harry Ferguson never saw the car race, as he died before it turned a wheel in anger.

The Rob Walker Team used the car in 2½-litre form for its first race - the 1961 British Empire Trophy at Silverstone – but it had to retire. Stirling Moss drove the car on its next two outings, the first being the British Grand Prix at Aintree, and the second the Oulton Park Gold Cup race in September 1961. It was here that the Ferguson-Climax P99 won its first and last Formula One race. Most of the vehicle's later competition work was restricted to the Tasman series of races and to hill-climbing. To this day, however, it holds the record for being the only four-wheel-drive car ever to win a Formula One race.

Several other interesting projects developed from the P99's success; there was a car built for the 1964 Indianapolis 500 Mile Race, and BRM, with the assistance of Ferguson, constructed their own experimental vehicle.

The R5 was the company's final development car. Two of them were built in the early sixties, both fitted with 2.2-litre engines, but one produced 111 b.h.p., whilst the other had over 50 b.h.p. more. The body's design was that of an estate, and with its advanced engineering specification it should have sold fairly well. However, at around the same time, Rover and Triumph released their new models, and thus the programme was abandoned.

The 1959 R5/2 Ferguson, with R4 just visible in the background

Ferguson R1 or 'Crab'

Although the Ferguson car never made it into production, several cars bearing the FF (Ferguson Formula) badge did. The Jensen brothers had got in touch with the company to ask them to develop a four-wheel-drive version of the C-V8. Work began, and when the C-V8 was replaced by the legendary Interceptor, a definitive model was born: the Interceptor FF.

GKN took over the manufacturing rights of the four-wheel-drive system in October 1969, and built several demonstration vehicles. In the early part of 1972, Tony Rolt founded FF Developments Ltd, and premises were acquired on the Siskin Drive Trading Estate near Baginton. Behind the scenes, FFD had been working on a new self-locking differential called a viscous coupling, which AMC of America used on their Eagle cars.

Over the years, many interesting projects have been undertaken by the company, and there should be many more to come. FF Developments are now based in Wolston, on the outskirts of the city, and still supply several very important firms.

Andy Rouse Engineering was formed in Daventry during 1981, after the sad decline of the Southam-based Broadspeed race-tuning shop. Rouse, now four times British Touring Car Champion, set up the company with Vic Drake (formally manager at Broadspeed) to carry on the work which Ralph Broad had started, but for personal reasons felt he could not continue. Andy's first championship was won with a Triumph Dolomite Sprint, and further links were forged with Coventry when he drove the big V12 racing Jaguar coupés in the mid-1970s.

The business moved to Progress Way in Coventry in 1983, with a short move to better workshops in Herald Way during August 1988. The company's engineering team have developed the Rover Vitesse, and more recently, variants of the Ford Sierra. At the moment, around twenty staff are employed, building about five cars a year, usually racing versions of the Sierra RS500 which push out something like 500 b.h.p. and cost around £75000 each.

The firm already supplies special components to clients all over the world. There is also a very successful Rouse racing team, and future plans include the conversion of standard road cars. Coventry's tradition of manufacturing top-quality racing machinery has not been so strong for many years.

Andy Rouse in action, driving one of his British Touring Car Championship cars

6

THE INDUSTRY TO THE SOUTH AND WEST

A LOOK AT THE CAR PRODUCERS ON THE SOUTH AND WEST SIDES OF THE CITY FROM THE EARLIEST DAYS OF THE INDUSTRY TO SPECIALIST COMPANIES OF TODAY.

Allard, Moor Street, 1898–1902
Rex, Osbourne Road, 1902–1914
Also included:
Acme, Lincoln Street, 1919

Clarendon, Moor Street, 1902–1905
Quadrant, Earlsdon, 1909
Arden, Balsall Common, 1912–1916
Buckingham, Holyhead Road, 1913–1923
Viking, Warwick Street, 1914
Aircraft, Shackleton Road, 1919–1930
Bramco, St Nicholas Street, 1921–1922
Carbodies, Holyhead Road, 1949–
John McGuire Racing, Fletchampstead Highway, 1977–
Auto-Forge Automobiles, Kirby Road, 1987–

The **Allard** Cycle Co. was originally formed in 1891, though it wasn't until 1899 that this Moor Street firm became involved in the motor trade, building De Dion-based tricycles and a Benz derivative known as the Express. Their 2½- and 3-h.p. voiturettes used single-cylinder 500-c.c. engines, again clearly based on De Dion practice. A tubular frame was used for the chassis, belt drives transmitted the power, and there was the option of either electric or hot-tube ignition. An oddity that Allard built in these early days was a narrow little *vis-à-vis* for two people.

Late in 1900 they built the belt-driven 'Charette', for a London-based company by the name of International. In 1902, a completely new 9-h.p. single-cylinder model made its debut. It featured a flitch-plate frame and a live axle. In June 1902 Allard got together with the Birmingham Motor Manufacturing and Supply Co., but the latter's Birmingham factory was sold; the business was absorbed into Rex and moved to Osbourne Road.

An Allard water-cooled engine (1900)

34

Rex's origins can be traced back to the 1880s, when William Pilkington founded a firm to produce weldless tubing for the cycle industry. After several mergers, the company Tubes Ltd was formed, although in 1899, Pilkington and his brother left to found the bicycle- and motorcycle-building business of The Rex Motor Manufacturing Co. Ltd.

1904 Rexette three-wheeler

The fusion with Allard and their subsequent move back to Coventry resulted in a wider range of vehicles for Rex, including some three-speed singles, and a 2.4-litre vertical-twin-cylinder car. Motor cars remained a sideline, as the company's staple products continued to be two-wheelers.

Rex built cars under a confusing variety of names: Ast-Rex, Rex-Remo, Airex and even Rex-Simplex (there was no connection between the latter and its German namesake). In 1903, the manufacture of pedal cycles ceased, and a new line of cars with Panhard-style radiators was introduced, their prices ranging from under £200 to over £400.

To complement these new models, a motorcycle-based tricar was produced. By 1904, this had been developed into the 'Rexette', which featured a car-type frame; a driver's seat replaced the saddle. The engine was a single-cylinder water-cooled unit, and drive was passed through a two-speed gearbox. With the adoption of wheel steering and three-

wheel brakes in 1905, it became even more car-like. For the following year, the Rexette was equipped with a transverse V-twin engine, and could be fitted with two-seater forecarriages.

The 12-h.p. two-cylinder Rex-Simplex car was sold during 1904 and 1905, although the tricar and motorcycle ranges continued to be the company's staple products. For 1906, the Ast-Rex was introduced. It featured a 3.7-litre four-cylinder Aster engine (hence its name), a three-speed gearbox and shaft drive. At £510, it didn't sell well, and was soon replaced by a new line of vehicles built under the Airex name.

When the Airex was announced towards the end of 1906, it was said to have a V4 engine. However, production models were fitted with 1.3-litre air-cooled V-twins, rated at 9/11 h.p. The specification included shaft drive, a three-speed gearbox, coil ignition and round-shaped radiators. A motorcycle-based Litette tricar was marketed at around the same time, though as its development continued, it became more and more like a two-wheeler.

For the 1908 season, Rex returned to building full-sized cars. Rex-Remo's, as they were known, were fairly straightforward T-headed four-cylinder machines, with shaft drive, magneto ignition and three-speed gearboxes. A honeycomb grille was used to conceal the gilled-tube radiators behind, and the last few examples were fitted with detachable wire wheels. They were made with a choice of either a 2.6- or a 2.8-litre engine. Production of this model ceased in 1911.

Apart from two other attempts at building cars, Rex remained in business by building motorcycles. There was a water-cooled V-twin cyclecar in 1912, and two years later a conventional light car, but both failed to get off the ground.

In 1922 Rex merged with **Acme,** another Coventry motorcycle manufacturer, and this new partnership lasted for six years. Acme had had a brief attempt at car manufacture in 1919, but soon lost interest in the project. The result of the new partnership saw the production of the Rex-Acme. Powered by various proprietary engines, the vehicle continued to be built for about six years. A revival of the Rex-Acme was staged in 1932 by the Mills-Fulford side-car company, but the venture survived for just one year. The last Rex motorcycles were built during 1933, and the company eventually faded away.

Incidentally, the Coventry Allard company bears no relation to the more famous London-based one. However, Fred Allard, the founder's son, was later to become the chief designer for Armstrong-Siddeley Motors.

The **Clarendon** Motor Car & Bicycle Co. Ltd built a typical two-seater voiturette. It used a single-cylinder engine rated at 7h.p., and had a shaft drive. On the other hand, the **Quadrant** Cycle Co. developed a bicycle gear which was applied so successfully to motor cars that in 1906 a subsidiary was formed to exploit its marketability. Quadrant are mentioned as motor manufacturers in the Coventry directories, but there is no evidence to support this claim.

Although the **Arden** appeared when the cyclecar boom was in full swing, this vehicle was more of a substantial light

1913 Arden; production had begun the year before

car. It was originally offered with a choice of two-cylinder engines: a water-cooled Alpha vertical-twin, or an air-cooled JAP V-twin. In 1914, the four-cylinder water-cooled Alpha engine was also added to the range, and a clover-leaf three-seater body now augmented the two-seaters. All Ardens were fitted with a three-speed gearbox, and had a shaft drive. When Arden ceased car production in 1916, E.A. Isherwood diverted his factory's production to war-work, making munitions. After the war they continued to build motorcycles, and began to manufacture proprietary engines for the trade, their sole selling agent being C.B. Harrison & Co. of Sheepcote Street, Birmingham.

The cyclecar designed by J.F. Buckingham was originally marketed as the Chota. The first model had an 8-h.p. single-cylinder air-cooled engine of Buckingham's own design and manufacture. This was later supplemented by a 12-h.p. V-twin. These vehicles had two forward speeds, and a final drive transmitted by belts. In September 1913 the marque name was changed to **Buckingham,** and a water-cooled single-cylinder model was added to the range.

Buckingham achieved a certain amount of competition success in the pre-war days, and production was raised to around fifteen units a week just before the hostilities began. After the war, the vehicles were built at the Alvis works in Holyhead Road. However, only a 10-h.p. V-twin was offered, similar in design to the earlier cars. This new model was too heavy, as well as being expensive, and thus never sold well. Production finally ended in 1923, and Buckingham himself would unfortunately be more famous for his designs for weapons of war than for cars.

The British **Viking** car was built in Warwick Street just before the outbreak of the First World War. It was usually powered by either a Mathis or a Ballot four-cylinder engine. The design of the springing system was borrowed from the early Lanchester cars, with long radius rods at the rear of the vehicle. A shaft final drive was employed, and the price was set at £160 for a two-seater model.

The **Aircraft** Motor & Engineering Works were listed among several known car manufacturers, though it is much more likely that they produced parts for cars, possibly engines. **Bramco** is another of those companies listed as motor manufacturers who seem never to have ever built a car. Based at No. 2, Radford Fields, St Nicholas Street, they were suppliers to the trade of engines and other components of various origins.

It was a former Daimler employee by the name of Bobby Jones who started the **Carbodies** business. The firm became an important supplier of light steel pressings to the trade during the thirties, as well as becoming a respected coach-building company. The BSA group took over Carbodies in 1954.

Carbodies have been making their famous range of FX black cabs since 1949. To date, nearly 80 000 of these taxis have been built. The earlier FX3 accounted for around 9000 of this total, with the familiar FX4 accounting for the remainder. Although the FX4 was introduced in 1959, many changes in detail have occurred to bring it up to date. The latest decision is to replace the old 2½-litre Land Rover diesel power unit with a Japanese Nissan one. This engine is more powerful, quieter and, linked to a matched four-speed

Viking light car (1914)

At the start of the ultimate test for any vehicle, a 14 148-mile journey from London to Sydney. The Carbodies taxi has been built under the flag of BSA, British Leyland and, more recently, London Taxis International (a member of the Manganese Bronze Group).

The author spotted this bright-yellow taxi outside the Casino at Monte Carlo!

Auto-Forge Sports at Coombe Abbey

automatic gearbox with selectable overdrive, makes town or motorway driving equally effortless.

An original FX4 replacement project concentrated on a Range Rover-based vehicle, but research indicated that it was the traditional black-cab shape that people liked. The new and much improved 'Fairway' model should stay in production for at least ten years. Its price on introduction (early in 1989) was in the region of £16000.

The firm known as **John McGuire Racing** has been in Coventry since it was set up in 1977 by John McGuire in workshops off the Stoney Stanton Road. Over the following eight years, many fibreglass and space-frame racing cars were built, including Minis, Lotus Esprits, Hillman Imps, Stilettos and even the odd Skoda or two, and they have found customers all over the world.

In 1983, McGuire moved to his new and current premises on Fletchampstead Highway, where he and his small team build and race Group One and Group A competition cars. At the moment, two BMW M3 Group A cars are in competition, and the team has nearly forty National Championship wins under its belt.

The kit-car world has come on in leaps and bounds over the past few years. Perhaps not surprisingly, Coventry plays host to one of the country's leading kit-car builders: **Auto-Forge Automobiles.** Formed in April 1987 by Dave Pepper, this small business had produced around sixty vehicles by 1989, with many more orders in the pipeline.

The car the firm builds is a very attractive two-door sports roadster based on a space-frame to Auto-Forge's own design. Power is usually supplied by Ford o.h.c. units, although the AF Sports has been produced in such a way that it will accept almost any straight four- or six-cylinder engine. The company hopes to expand and to supply only complete hand-built cars in the future.

7

THE PARKSIDE-BASED COMPANIES

PARKSIDE HAS PLAYED HOST TO SOME VERY FAMOUS FIRMS. IT SAW SIDDELEY DEVELOP INTO ONE OF THE MOST RESPECTED NAMES IN THE TRADE, AND FADE AWAY AS ARMSTRONG SIDDELEY. MAUDSLAY, ANOTHER OF THE GREAT MARQUES, ALSO HAD ITS WORKS WHERE NOW THE FLAG OF ROLLS-ROYCE PROUDLY FLIES.

Siddeley through to *Armstrong Siddeley, 1902–1960*

Also included:
Stoneleigh, 1912–1930   *Maudslay, 1901–1926*
Velox, 1902–1904   *Motor Radiator, 1912*

The **Siddeley** company was founded by John Davenport Siddeley, who was born in Cheadle Hulme in 1866. In his youth he was a keen cyclist, and rode from John O'Groats to Land's End on a machine built by Humber, the company he would later join as a draughtsman. His work took him to Dunlop in Ireland, and by 1899 he had his own tyre-manufacturing firm, the Clipper Tyre Co., based in Fleet Street, Coventry.

During the famous Thousand Miles Trial of 1900, Siddeley drove a 6-h.p. Parisien Daimler, and just a year later, having started importing and selling Peugeot and Renault vehicles, he began marketing his own vehicles from the Wolseley factory in Birmingham. Sales were handled from an office in Westminster directly opposite the Wolseley Tool & Motor Co. works.

A delightful picture of J.D. Siddeley with one of his creations, dating from around 1904. This is thought to be the car on display at the Coventry branch of the Rolls-Royce Heritage Trust.

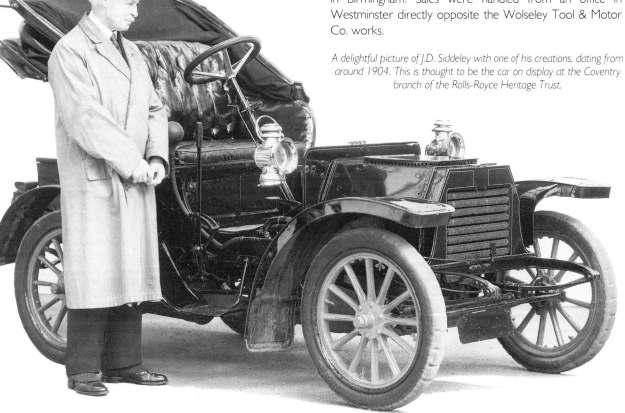

The Siddeley Autocar Co. was formed during the early part of 1902 and was based next door to Rover in Garfield Road. Not surprisingly, the newly formed company's first car was based on an established vehicle. In fact, only the body was locally made, the rest of the machine being imported from Peugeot.

In 1903, Siddeley approached Vickers, Son & Maxim, the then owners of Wolseley, for help with the construction of his cars, the components for which were made at the Wolseley factory in Birmingham. By 1904, the Austin-designed horizontal-engined 6 h.p. and the Siddeley-designed four-cylinder 18 h.p. were joined by a twin-cylinder 12 h.p., a four-cylinder 32 h.p. of 5½ litres, and another of 7 litres. The company also built a 100-h.p. racing car for the 1905 Gordon Bennett race, but unfortunately a wheel came off, and the car failed to finish.

Wolseley and Siddeley amalgamated in 1905 to form the Wolseley-Siddeley Motor Co. Siddeley was made sales manager, whilst Herbert Austin became works manager. Towards the end of the year, Austin resigned to make his own cars, leaving Siddeley the post of general manager. In the following years, he would produce an elegant and popular line of vehicles, including small tourers, large limousines, buses and ambulances.

Siddeley moved back to Coventry in 1909, when he joined the Parkside-based Deasy outfit as works manager. Because the Siddeley name belonged to Wolseley until 1910, it wasn't until the following year that it could be used again.

Eventually, the Siddeley-Deasy Motor Co. would be formed.

The Deasy company had been formed in February 1906 by Captain Henry Deasy, a famous racing driver, while he still owned H.H.P. Deasy & Co., importers of Martini and Rochet-Schneider vehicles. The Parkside firm had bought the old buildings previously occupied by the ill-fated Iden company. Further buildings were soon built, and the works were run by Edmund Lewis, the designer of Rover cars. Captain Deasy severed his links with the company in the same year that Siddeley joined, and within a few months the latter was appointed as the new managing director.

The Deasy-designed chassis, with engines of 4½, 8½ and 12 litres, were soon superseded by Siddeley's own designs. The old rounded Siddeley radiator was replaced by a coffin-shaped bonnet, with the radiator itself being mounted by the scuttle, following the fashion set by the earlier Renault vehicles.

These new Deasy models had engine capacities ranging from 3.3 to 7.5 litres, and all components were bought in from other companies. Engines, for instance, came from such famous names as Austro-Daimler, Rover and the Lockhurst Lane-based White & Poppe. The legendary Knight sleeve-valve unit (as used by British Daimlers), was also employed for some of the larger engines. By tightening up the whole operation at Parkside, chassis production was soon up to six a week.

Although the Siddeley name was once again free for use by 1911, it wasn't until the following year that it appeared in

1908 Deasy 35-h.p. Cabriolet

a marque name. The newly formed Siddeley-Deasy Motor Co. had three four-cylinder cars and two six-cylinder versions in its range, and the situation would remain the same until the outbreak of the First World War.

At the same time as the Siddeley-Deasy company was founded, a subsidiary under the name of **Stoneleigh** was formed. Only economy cars and commercial vehicles would be marketed under this name, Siddeley-Deasy being aimed more at the quality end of the scale. The first Stoneleigh cars were probably the 11.9-h.p. models produced by BSA. Interest in the project soon faded, and only small lorries and a fourteen-seat bus chassis continued to be built. The largest order for the 1½- and 2-ton Stoneleigh trucks came from Imperial Russia, where at least 100 vehicles ended up, along with several Siddeley-Deasy staff cars, ambulances and field kitchens. Oddly, Stoneleighs were never very popular in the United Kingdom, so it is perhaps surprising that Armstrong-Siddeley revived car production in 1922. Stoneleigh models were still being produced right up until around 1924, although they were little more than cyclecars by then.

The firm's war-work consisted mainly of building Army vehicles, airframes and aero-engines. Development of the latter culminated in the design and production of the world-famous Puma engine. By the end of the war, the design of a new 30-h.p. model was well under way. Talks between Siddeley's and Daimler about a possible merger had collapsed, but negotiations between Armstrong-Whitworth and Siddeley-Deasy finally came to fruition, and the **Armstrong Siddeley** Motor Co. was formed in May 1919, as a subsidiary of the Armstrong-Whitworth Development Co. Ltd.

The 30 h.p. was introduced in 1919 as the first Armstrong Siddeley car. It had a 5-litre engine and, despite a post-war slump, sold at a steady rate. Two years later a smaller 18-h.p. version was launched. Both cars had tourer or saloon bodies of great strength and comfort. They soon developed a good reputation, and attracted a clientele that would include royalty.

During the early 1920s Siddeley tried to get into the military-vehicle field, without much success. However, the attempt did put him in contact with Colonel W.G. Wilson, the designer of the Wilson-Pilcher epicyclic transmission car. The patents for the Wilson gearbox would eventually be acquired by Armstrong Siddeley, and the subsidiary company Self-Changing Gears (which still exists in Coventry) was set up.

By 1925, the additional 14-h.p. model announced a couple of years earlier was beginning to sell fairly well, and all three models had been improved. It was the manufacture of aircraft engines, though, that ensured the survival of the company during the lean years of the twenties. However, in 1926 Siddeley was still able to buy back his old business, for the staggering sum of £1.5 million (this did include the aircraft manufacturing rights, as well as another aircraft company, A.V. Roe Ltd).

The styling of the 30- and 18-h.p. cars was very much that of the dreadnought type. The massive 'V' radiator was drawn by the famous artist Gordon Crosby, as was the upright Sphinx that we now associate with the company. Both

1912 Siddeley-Deasy Althorp Special Cabriolet

One of the last of the marque: a 1924 Stoneleigh light car

12-h.p. coach-built 1930 Siddeley saloon

vehicles were suitable for all kinds of modifications; one 30-h.p. model was stripped down and raced at Brooklands, but more common adaptations included conversions to buses, ambulances, hearses, pick-up trucks, motor caravans and limousines.

The 14-h.p. model, built between 1923 and 1929, was fitted with a flat radiator. This vehicle was augmented in 1928 by the country's smallest straight six – the 12 h.p. This model unfortunately stayed in production for only about three years, its relatively short life being due mainly to its distinct lack of performance.

A major sales drive was attempted in 1932, with the launch of a whole new range of cars. Four rally touring cars were prepared for the Alpine Trials of that year, and gave an impressive performance, but it was the replacement for the ageing 30-h.p. model that probably gave the biggest boost to the company, the touring models being quite capable of speeds in excess of 100 m.p.h. Sadly, Rolls-Royce, Bentley and Daimler had the touring-car market pretty well cornered, and only 253 of the Siddeley Specials, as they were called, were ever built.

In 1935 Sir John Siddeley (he had been knighted in 1932, and became Lord Kenilworth five years later), sold his holdings in the Armstrong Siddeley Development Corporation to Hawkers, but not before the 'V' radiator was fitted across the range, and minor improvements on the Siddeley Special gave it a Mark II designation. Both of Sir John's sons stayed with the company, but from this point onwards, economy would become a major factor in the production of the vehicles.

As with so many of the Coventry factories during the Second World War, Armstrong Siddeley were a prime target for German air raids. The Parkside works were heavily bombed, but many airframes, aero-engines, torpedo gyroscopes and over 30000 tank gearboxes managed to leave the factory before the hostilities ceased.

Almost as soon as the war had ended, the post-war range of cars was put on the market. The first model to emerge was the drop-head four-seater called the Hurricane. This was a development of the 16 h.p. introduced just before the outbreak of war. The Lancaster six-light saloon soon followed, and both cars were fitted with six-cylinder engines and independent front suspension. Midway through 1946, a hard-top version of the Hurricane, the Typhoon, was also launched.

The Sapphire 346 was introduced in 1953, the year in which Lord Kenilworth died, and it was to be the mainstay of the Armstrong Siddeley range for another five years. It had a six-cylinder, 3435-c.c. engine and was capable of nearly 100 m.p.h., depending on whether the four- or six-light body was fitted. The engine design was an innovation, with a valve layout that enabled the use of hemispherical combustion chambers and inclined valves, but employed only one camshaft.

The new four-light models came in 1954. Both had an engine capacity of 2.3 litres, but one used four cylinders, the other six. These were to be known as the Sapphire 234 and 236 respectively.

The final production car to be built by Armstrong Siddley was the Star Sapphire. The 4-litre engine was coupled to a Borg Warner automatic gearbox, and the car proved to be both faster and smoother than the 346 model. It also had more comfort and interior space, and was lavishly equipped to keep up with the competition. A limousine version was made available on a slightly longer chassis, though very few were ever sold before the company ceased car production in 1960.

Sir Malcolm Campbell's 4.9-litre Siddeley Special

1950 Armstrong Siddeley Hurricane

The distinguished 1958 Armstrong Siddeley Star Sapphire. Note the Coventry-issued number-plate (DU).
Other letter-combinations include HP, KV, RW, VC and WK.

Thereafter, Armstrong Siddeley concentrated on aerospace work, the production of a few power trucks, and Sunbeam Alpine bodies for Rootes, being the sum total of their involvement with automobiles. The Rolls-Royce Heritage Trust, also based at Parkside, now looks after the oldest surviving example of a Siddeley, as well as many of the company records.

The first **Velox** cars were originally built in a part of the Amalgamated Tyre Co. works at Parkside. The 1902 model had a 10-h.p. two-cylinder Abeille engine, a four-speed gearbox and a shaft drive. For the next year's trading season, two new models were built: a 10-h.p. four-cylinder car with a Forman engine, and the Miniature Velox, which was a very low two-seater powered by a single-cylinder Aster engine of 4½ h.p. Both of these vehicles also had a shaft drive.

Near the end of 1903, another four-cylinder car was added to the range but only twenty-one of these new 20-h.p. models were ever built. Fifteen more had been in the course of construction, but unfortunately the company had to close down before any more could be sold.

The **Maudslay** Motor Co. was a branch of the famous engineering firm which had been building marine engines for many years. Indeed, Maudslay engines powered a good percentage of Royal Navy warships. They had also built a steam carriage in 1833. In 1899 the original business in London collapsed, but not before an internal-combustion marine engine department had been set up in Coventry. After the fall of the parent company, it was re-formed in

1901 as the Maudslay Motor Co. founded by Cyril, Charles and Walter Henry Maudslay, cousins of Reginald Maudslay, who promptly formed his own Standard car company.

Their first car was designed by Alexander Craig in 1901. It had a 20-h.p. three-cylinder engine with an overhead camshaft, a four-speed gearbox and a final drive of double chains. Many of the early Maudslays had bodies which could be converted from an open brake style for use in warmer weather into a closed station omnibus.

In 1904, a larger three-cylinder car of a 25-h.p. rating was introduced as well as two six-cylinder models of 40 and 60 h.p. respectively. The engines in the latter vehicles were exactly double the size of the 20 and 25 h.p. By the end of the season, very few 'sixes' had been built, so in the following year Maudslay introduced a new range of four-cylinder cars, on which they would standardize until the outbreak of the First World War, although one 16/20-h.p. three-cylinder model was made until 1906.

The large round radiator had been a feature of the company's cars from around 1905. There was already a growing line of commercial vehicles, and both stationary and marine engines stayed in production.

Until 1910, it was the large 'fours' of 20/30 and 35/45 h.p. that continued in production, shaft drive making an appearance in 1908. In 1909 a new 17-h.p. car was announced, and, by the following year, it had a silent-chain-driven gearbox. The larger models were gradually discontinued; by 1914, only the 17 h.p., known at the factory as

1905 20-h.p. Maudslay limousine

Maudslay 15/80 chassis

A superb 1910 32-h.p. Maudslay tourer

the 'Sweet Seventeen', was being made. This was to be Maudslay's most successful car, at least in sales terms. All of these cars had retained the single-o.h.c. layout for their engines, something the company had championed from their earliest days.

Maudslay's interesting slide-valve engine project had to be abandoned with the coming of war. Instead the factory concentrated on supplying lorries to the Ministry, as well as carrying out subcontract work on aero-engines. Owing to the lack of space at Parkside, a lot of this took place at the nearby Rover works.

It wasn't until 1923 that the first of the post-war cars left the Parkside works, the delay being caused by full order books for commercial vehicles. This very advanced vehicle, known as the 15/80, had an engine of 1991 c.c., with twin overhead camshafts and six cylinders. Perrot four-wheel brakes were also a feature, but even though it was proudly

displayed at Olympia, the car never went into production. The prototype was destroyed in a fire, and nothing was ever heard of the second car.

It was then that Maudslay's decided to concentrate on heavy commercial vehicles, despite the excellent reputation they had gained as manufacturers of fine cars. The Coventry Corporation ordered several Maudslay buses, but the company moved to a new site near Alcester just after the 1939–45 war, thus losing their links with the city.

There was a merger with Crossley and AEC in 1948, although the Maudslay name was still used for another ten years. After this, it was mainly components that the company built. The year 1972 saw the business bought out by Rockwell, but the company still exists today, as Rockwell-Maudslay.

The firm known as the **Motor Radiator** Manufacturing Co. used to advertise themselves as motor manufacturers, though no records have been found to substantiate this claim. All that has been found concerning the company's activities is an entry in the 1912 Motor Show Catalogue, where their stand showed several brass and silver-plated radiator grilles, as well as a pair of sample bonnets.

Engine-building at the Maudslay factory, c. 1910

8

OF METEORS AND CRESTED EAGLES

ALVIS AND ROVER HAVE HAD CLOSE LINKS FOR MANY YEARS, ALTHOUGH THE TWO FIRMS HAVE EXPERIENCED QUITE DIFFERENT HISTORIES.

Rover, *Garfield Road, 1904–1945*
Alvis, *Holyhead Road, 1920–1967*

John Kemp Starley

James Starley, 'the father of the safety cycle', started his career with the famous Coventry Sewing Machine Co. He had founded the business in 1861 with his partner, Josiah Turner. When the company name was changed in 1868 to the Coventry Machinists Co. Ltd, the firm's manufacture of sewing-machines continued, but the production of several other items, including the French-designed velocipede, gave Starley an opening into the world of the bicycle (see *also* Singer). When Starley left in 1870 to set up his own company, he took with him his foreman, William Hillman, and his nephew, John Kemp Starley, also joined the new outfit.

In 1877 John Kemp Starley left his uncle to start his own business, known as Starley & Sutton. The original factory was the Meteor Works in West Orchard, and it was here, as early as 1884, that Starley first applied the Rover trade-name to some of his machines. When William Sutton left the partnership in 1888, the company was re-established as J.K. Starley & Co. Ltd. The bicycle boom was well under way by now, and Starley was one of the leading Coventry manufacturers. 1896 saw the firm go public, with the formation of the Rover Cycle Co. Ltd.

The monument erected in recognition of the work of James Starley stands today in Warwick Row, Coventry.

J.K. Starley had designed and built an electric car in 1888, but Rover were far more famous in the earlier days for their bicycles and motor bikes. James Starley died young in 1901, when his nephew's company were on the verge of producing their powered machines. Compared to some of the other cycle firms, however, the Rover company branched into the motor trade quite late. The first tricars had appeared in 1903, and within only two years these had evolved into their definitive form of wheel-steered vehicles, powered by water-cooled twin-cylinder engines.

It was in the summer of 1904 that the first production Rover four-wheeler was announced. Edmund Lewis, an ex-

THE ROVER
100 GUINEAS ONLY.

6 h.p. ROVER CAR. 100 Gns.

Rover Cars will be shown at
the Manchester Show on Messrs.
Newton, Bennett and Carlisle's
Stand.

THE ROVER CO., Ltd., Meteor Works, COVENTRY.

LONDON—19, Holborn Viaduct, E.C.
    Garage, 3, 4, and 5, Harpur
    Mews, Theobald's Rd., W.C.
    STRATFORD, E.:
    399, High Street.
CROYDON—9a, George Street.
DUBLIN—23, Westmoreland Street.
BELFAST—81, King Street.
MANCHESTER—7, St. Mary's Gate.

MANCHESTER—Newton, Bennett and
    Carlisle, Ltd., King Street W.
LIVERPOOL—35, Bold Street.
NEWCASTLE-ON-TYNE—
    116, Northumberland Street.
LEEDS—Guildford Street.
BIRMINGHAM—Victoria Square.
CARDIFF—9, Working Street.
BRIDGWATER—Bridgwater Motor
    Co., Ltd., Eastover.

BRIGHTON—Hammond and Sons,
    Waterloo Street, Hove.
NORWICH—Mann, Egerton and Co.,
    Ltd., Prince of Wales Road.
DARLINGTON—Cleveland Car Co.,
    Cleveland Bridge Works.
GLASGOW—Gibbon & Co., West Nile
    Street.
EDINBURGH—W. Flint, Hanover
    Street.

Art Catalogue No. I, with all particulars, free on request.

Daimler employee, was the man responsible for its design, and he decided to use a tubular backbone frame, an 8-h.p. single-cylinder engine and a camshaft brake arrangement. The wire-and-bobbin steering was soon replaced by a far better rack-and-pinion system. A smaller, 6-h.p. version was introduced to complement this vehicle, although it was one of the original 8-h.p. cars that Dr Jefferson used on his pioneering drive from London to Constantinople. In 1906 the Rover Motor Co. Ltd was formed with a capital of £100 000.

The first four-cylinder Rover was the 16/20-h.p. model, featuring a 3.1-litre engine and shaft drive. It was one of these cars that would be victorious in the 1907 Isle of Man Tourist Trophy Race, driven by Ernest Courtis, who won the race with a lead of over twelve minutes. The famous shield-shaped radiator was introduced in 1907, and this, in various forms, was to be a feature until well after production moved from Coventry. By now, a monobloc 10/12-h.p. car had joined the range, and Hawkins & Peake – local coach-builders who had previously built bodies for both Rover and Humber – were acquired by the company.

By 1908, the 8-h.p. model's gear-change had moved from the column to the right-hand side of the vehicle. The single-cylinder and 20-h.p. cars were augmented by conventional

L-head models of 1.6 and 2.5 litres in 1909, Rover's own detachable wheels becoming optional for the following year.

Knight sleeve-valve engines were employed on an alternative version of the 8-h.p. model, and because of this it retailed at a much higher price. A Knight power unit was also used on the new vertical-twin 12-h.p. car of 1.9 litres. However, 1912 was the last year that Rover marketed their singles and twins. The new era began with the Clegg-designed 2.3-litre four-cylinder monobloc engine. This was adopted in the new 12-h.p. model, which sold for £350. It featured a worm drive, electric lighting, inlet ports that were cast into the cylinder head, and a water-jacketed carburettor. By 1914 this would be the only car that Rover listed in their sales literature. Later on, it would be known as the Fourteen, and the headlamps would be attached to the radiator shell. Production of this model finally ceased in 1924.

During the war years, Rover built 12/16-h.p. Sunbeams for the Ministry of War, as well as a batch of lorries for Maudslay, but soon reverted back to economy-class vehicles once the hostilities came to an end. The Eight made its debut in 1920. Originally powered by a 1-litre air-cooled flat-twin engine, it retained the 12-h.p.-type worm final drive. It was also built under licence by Peter & Moritz, a German-based company. When production of the Eight ended in 1925, the price had dropped from £300 to just over half that figure. The cars were built at the newly acquired ex-munitions factory at Tyseley, Birmingham, but were shipped back to Coventry to have the bodies fitted.

The Eight's successor was an o.h.v. water-cooled in-line four known as the 9/20. This cost in the region of £215, and had acquired front-wheel brakes by the second year of its

manufacture. A detachable hard-top coupé body became available in 1927, but then it was replaced by the 1.2-litre Ten, also fitted with worm drive.

A big 3½-litre six-cylinder car announced in 1924 unfortunately never made it into production, though Rover did build some very advanced cars between 1925 and 1928. The four-cylinder o.h.c. engines of 2.1 and 2.5 litres designed by Peter Poppe (of White & Poppe) featured hemispherical combustion chambers. They gave the company some competition success, but were very expensive to produce.

The company's breakthrough with bigger cars came with the straightforward 2-litre o.h.v. bevel-drive six-cylinder model. This sold well at £410, and was eventually developed into the stylish Light Six of 1930 vintage. It was this model which beat the Blue Train in a race across France, although

1929 Rover 10/25

A Clegg-designed 1921 12-h.p. tourer

the same engine was also used to propel a large limousine. By now, a gentleman by the name of Spencer Wilks, previously with the Hillman company, had taken the position of general manager. It was not long before he was given the post of managing director, and, without doubt, it was Wilks who saved Rover from oblivion.

A cheap and very basic rear-engined car, known as the Scarab, was due to be announced for the 1931 Motor Show, but the cautious management decided against its launch at the last moment, and the vehicle never went into production. The year 1931 saw V-radiators, lowered chassis and conventionally mounted headlamps, with a line of cars ranging from the Ten, costing just £189, to the 2.6-litre Meteor 20, priced at £398. The latter was developed into a 90-m.p.h. sports model, which proved very popular. The 1.4-litre Pilot was added to the range in the following year.

Factories were rationalized under Wilks. The old Meteor Works were sold in 1932, and production was concentrated on the Helen Street premises, which were renamed 'The New Meteor Works'. Production rose, and, after several years of serious losses in the late twenties, the company finally began to show a profit again.

Spencer Wilks entered the 1933 RAC Rally along with his brother Maurice, who was by now head of the engineering department. Maurice managed to gain third place in his class, while Spencer won the coachwork competition for 10- to 16-h.p. cars with his Rover coupé bodied by Carbodies.

A cheap Ten was still being listed in 1933, but this was the year in which Rover started to concentrate on the quality end of the market, a tradition the marque continues to this day. The 1934 models had four-speed gearboxes, o.h.v. engines and spiral-bevel final drives. The range consisted of a new 1.4-litre Ten, a four-cylinder Twelve, a 1.6-litre six-cylinder Fourteen, and a 16-h.p. Meteor saloon. The company tried hydraulic brakes for a while, but soon reverted back to a mechanical type of actuation.

In 1937 all models were restyled (with the exception of the Ten, which wasn't touched until two years later), but the big cars were still offered, a 2.1-litre 16 h.p. and a new 2½-litre Speed 20 being listed.

After the war production of all Rover vehicles was moved to nearby Solihull. This new site had been created through the Shadow Factory scheme, as had the Rootes Ryton works. The new Meteor Works were sold in 1945.

1938 Rover Fourteen saloon

The wartime development of gas-turbine and jet engines continued through the fifties and sixties, and the findings were applied to experimental cars and, later, to racing cars. In 1965 the Alvis company was acquired, further strengthening Rover's links with Coventry, but it would not be long until both firms became just another part of the massive British Leyland empire.

At least one Rover car will continue to be produced in the city well into the 1990s: the Rover limousine built by Park Sheet Metal. Although the project very much belongs to Startins of Birmingham, who thought of the idea, it is due to the skills of this Coventry company that the dream of a stretched Rover 827Si saloon became a reality. A further build capacity could well be built in Birmingham at a later date, but, for the time being at least, the Rover car still has a place in its home town.

The story of the Red Triangle begins on the Holyhead Road in 1920. The original works were much smaller than the factory now used for the production of military vehicles, and were situated on the other side of the Alvis bridge. The present **Alvis** factory was built in 1935; during a bombing raid in the Second World War, the first site was completely destroyed and is now used only for storage purposes.

The company was founded by Thomas George John, a former naval architect and aero-engine designer at Siddeley-Deasy, who was born in 1880 in Argylle Street, Pembroke Dock. The first Alvis car was completed in March 1920. This model, the 10/30, went into production in July of the same year. It is interesting to note that, at that time, the apex of the triangle which forms the company's badge was at the top of the Alvis name, the opposite way round to its position today. The badge was also winged, and had either a green or a blue background.

The 10/30, despite its high price, soon became very popular, and by the following year expansion was necessary. On 14 December 1921 the company was renamed the Alvis Car & Engineering Co. Ltd. Shortly afterwards, Alvis took over the manufacture of the Buckingham cyclecar from another Coventry firm, though no more than thirty were ever built at the Alvis works, the cyclecar's premature end being hastened by the introduction of the Austin Seven midway through 1922.

During the winter of 1922, work commenced on a new racing car, and by the spring of 1923 the vehicle was being tested in the early hours around the streets of Coventry. This became one of the finest British light cars of the vintage period – the 12/50. These were exciting times for the Alvis company. Victory came at Brooklands in the 200 Mile Race, which was quite an achievement, because the Alvis car was based on the standard 12/50, whereas other factory teams, such as Fiat, fielded out-and-out racers. Had the 12/50 not been such a success, the Alvis marque would almost certainly have crumbled, as the coach-builders Cross & Ellis had brought the business into the hands of the receiver. Fortunately, the reputation of the 12/50 had spread, encouraging creditors to supply further finance.

A little while later, and some thirty years before the Mini, Alvis adopted front-wheel drive, first for a sprint car, then for racing, and finally for production cars. Several cars with either

Developed for the Le Mans races, the Rover B.R.M. was powered by a gas-turbine engine and bodied by Motor Panels in 18-gauge Elektron. Between 1963 and 1965 several top drivers put the car through its paces, with fairly good results.

The prototype Rover limousine outside the works where it was built

The Alvis factory, Holyhead Road. It will be a sad day when the building is demolished and Coventry loses another landmark. The proposed new site is at Walsgrave, backing on to the M6.

Racing Alvis 12/50 with polished aluminium bodywork

*The works entry of front-wheel-drive Alvis cars ready for the 1930
Tourist Trophy Race*

four- or eight-cylinder engines were built between 1925 and 1930, but the Depression forced Alvis to kill off the project after just 140 cars.

To the 12/50 range was added a new six-cylinder 14/75 engine. It had a capacity of 1870 c.c. and was fitted into the existing chassis. It was from this vehicle that the Silver Eagle (1929) and other, later, six-cylinder cars were developed.

Between 1932 and 1936 the company's main income came from the Speed\20, a development of the Silver Eagle. Few cars with an engine of 2½ litres could match the performance of this vehicle, and it was later learned that this was the car that Rolls-Royce considered to be their main competitor in the 20-h.p. range. Luxury was now as important as high performance for Alvis, and it was around

Alvis Speed 25 with coachwork by Vanden Plas

this time that the company put in a bid for the ailing Lagonda business. Unfortunately, their bid of £35 000 was too low, and the marque was sold to Alan Good.

The early thirties saw Alvis, along with several other companies, looking into ways of improving the 'crash' gearbox. Daimler of course came up with the fluid flywheel, whereas by 1933 Alvis, having first designed something called the 'automatic traffic clutch', had fitted the first ever all-synchromesh gearbox into a Speed 20 chassis.

After the Firefly came the Crested Eagle. This car was aimed more at the carriage sector of the market, and was fitted with independent front suspension – the first Alvis production car to have such an arrangement since the front-wheel drive vehicles. Production of this vehicle lasted until the outbreak of the Second World War.

In October 1935 a new 3½-litre car was announced. This vehicle, considered by many to be the best of the pre-war cars, was named the Speed 25. Indeed, Sir Malcolm Campbell praised the performance of this lovely car while he was the World Land Speed Record holder! It was also around this time that negotiations were completed for the company to enter the aero-engine industry (see Appendices).

In June 1936 the company was renamed for the third time, becoming Alvis Ltd. By now talks were well under way for supplying the Ministry of War with armoured vehicles – a sign of things to come (see Appendices).

A short time afterwards, George Lanchester (of the famous engineering family) joined the company as assistant chief engineer of the car section. The Silver Crest was largely his work, and now another new car appeared: the 12/70. The Speed 25 had replaced the Speed 20, and the 3½-litre engine had been enlarged to 4.3 litres, further improving the already good performance.

Throughout the war, Alvis worked hard, building, machining and overhauling a vast array of military machines and equipment. T.G. John retired in 1944, and Captain G.T. Smith-Clarke took over the helm. Later, J.J. Parkes would become managing director.

Just after the war, Alan Good gave Alvis the chance to buy Lagonda for £75 000, but the offer was quickly declined, as Alvis had already laid its post-war plans. The first new post-war Alvis to appear was the Fourteen, later typed the TA14. This car made its debut in 1946, and was soon followed by the TB14, a roadster version of the same vehicle.

Superb Alvis TA14, with Carbodies coachwork, outside Broadcasting House, London

The TC21/100 or 'Grey Lady'

It wasn't until March 1950 that the company showed its next car. The 3 litre (or Type TA21) saw several changes, developing into the TB21, then the TC21 and TC21/100 (Grey Lady). This last model attracted the attention of a coach-builder named Graber, and the TC108G, with Graber coachwork, was announced in October 1955. Although this was certainly one of the most beautiful cars of the series, because of its high price only sixteen were ever produced.

Around three years later, Alvis decided to build a much less expensive Graber-style vehicle. This was achieved by using Park Ward to make the bodies to Graber designs. The vehicle was based on the earlier models, and was designated the TD21.

The TD continued in production until the introduction of the TE21 at the 1964 Motor Show. A final revision was made two years later with the coming of the TF21, and this was to be the last of the Alvis cars. It was also the fastest standard car of the marque, being able to reach 126 m.p.h. with relative ease.

The last of the TF21s left the factory in September 1967, and although no more Alvis cars were built, the name still lives on, as Alvis became a major producer of armoured vehicles. Shortly after a merger with Rover, the company became part of British Leyland. One mid-engined prototype sports car was built by Alvis, using a Rover 3½-litre V8. However this failed to fit in with the BL marketing philosophy, and was scrapped. Once released from Leyland, Alvis were sold to United Scientific Holdings for the staggering sum of £27 million in 1981.

The famous Red Triangle is still a symbol of quality, but production now concentrates almost exclusively on armoured vehicles. The Holyhead Road factory stands as a monument to the superb cars it once produced.

Examples of the first and last Alvis cars: the 10/30 and the TF21

9

LORD NUFFIELD IN COVENTRY

WILLIAM MORRIS, LATER LORD NUFFIELD, OWNED SEVERAL VERY IMPORTANT MARQUES. MANY OF THEM DEPENDED ON HIS COVENTRY BRANCHES TO SUPPLY THEIR BIGGER FACTORIES OUTSIDE THE CITY.

Morris and *Hotchkiss*

Riley, Durbar Avenue, 1898–1938
Also included:
Autovia, Midland Road, 1936–1938

William Morris was born in Comer Gardens, Worcester, on 10 October 1877. When the Morris family moved back to Oxford, William was the eldest of seven children. Soon after he left school, he set up his own bicycle repair business. It quickly developed, and within a couple of years he was assembling his own machines.

Morris became works manager of the Oxford Automobile & Cycle Agency in 1903, though this position was to be short-lived, as the company was bankrupt in less than a year. He went back to building and marketing bicycles, as well as selling the odd car.

For several years, Morris had been seriously considering becoming a car manufacturer. He made many contacts in the Midlands, and, in 1912, founded a company: W.R.M. Motors. In the early years, engines were supplied by White & Poppe, but eventually American mass-production priced the Coventry company out of the market.

In 1923 William Morris acquired the Hollick & Pratt coach-building firm. He had already bought **Hotchkiss,** the engine-builders. This came about when his American engine suppliers (Continental of Detroit) stopped making their V-type unit. White & Poppe were fully occupied at the time, so Morris decided to purchase his own engine manufacturers.

The Coventry Hotchkiss company was a British offshoot of the famous French firm, established during the First World War to make engines in the United Kingdom. Their units powered many Morris and BSA light cars, but before Morris acquired the company in 1920, they had experimented with a small car of their own. It used an air-cooled 1080-c.c. V-twin o.h.v. engine and a three-speed gearbox, mounted into an early Morris Oxford chassis. Unfortunately, the vehicle never went into production.

William Morris (later Lord Nuffield)

The Morris Engines works

By 1929, Morris Engines (as Hotchkiss were now known), had opened up a new plant at the northern end of the city, at Courthouse Green. This new works would eventually become the focus of the company's operations in Coventry, leading to the closure of the old Hotchkiss premises. These engine plants would play a crucial part in the success of the Morris group. Further links with Coventry came through the purchase of the **Riley** marque in 1938.

The Riley family had been established in Coventry long before it became involved in the motor trade. Originally, the Riley name was associated with weaving, but with the decline of this industry, William Riley decided to acquire the Bonnick cycle-manufacturing company. This was in 1890, and by May 1896 the Riley name had appeared, replacing that of Bonnick.

It was just over three years later that the first motor-powered Riley appeared. The Royal Riley Quadricycle was exhibited at the National Cycle Show at Crystal Palace in 1899. Several tricycle and quadricycle models followed, with motorcycles coming as a natural progression.

In 1903 a new company, the Riley Engine Co., was announced. Previously, engines had been bought in from either De Dion-Bouton or, more locally, from MMC. It wasn't until 1905 that the first real Riley cars went into production, although a prototype had been built and sold about seven years earlier. The Riley 9 h.p., as it was known, was powered by a V-twin engine of the design previously employed on the tricycle.

Although the company had started life in King Street, in the latter half of 1906 they moved into bigger premises in Aldbourne Road, off Widdrington Road, but still within Coventry.

Two years after the 9 h.p. had been launched, and well received, Riley tried out a new model, with a more powerful engine and a larger seating capacity. The prototype was known in the factory as 'Old Midnight' because of the hours that went into it. Eventually, Riley were satisfied, and the 12/18 h.p. was released.

At the 1908 Olympia Motor Show, the company introduced another new model, the 10 h.p. It was basically the same as the 12/18, but with detail changes to the engine and chassis; it was also a two-seater, unlike its four-seater predecessor.

In mid-1909 there came news of a sleeve-valve four-cylinder engine designed by Percy Riley. He later experimented with a 17/30-h.p. unit of this design, but eventually sold the patent to an American company and came down in favour of poppet-valves. This engine was the first Riley unit to use the four-cylinder in-line design.

Gradually the 9 h.p. was discontinued, more attention being paid to the two larger cars. The 12/18 h.p. became available with either two- or four-seater coachwork.

By now, the detachable-wheel section of the company was becoming so lucrative that it was decided to concentrate solely on wheels. In 1912, over 180 companies were using their wire wheels, so the thinking behind this was not unsound. Fortunately, however, the Riley brothers continued to build motor cars.

The Riley Motor Manufacturing Co., as it was now known,

1904 Riley tricar on the London to Brighton run

1908 Riley 12/18 with four-seater coachwork

exhibited a totally new car at the 1913 Motor Show: the 17 h.p. This new model used a four cylinder in-line engine of 2951 c.c., and was the first production car from the marque not to use the faithful V-twin. Obviously, the 17/30-h.p. engine was a result of the experiments conducted by Percy Riley around four years earlier.

At the same time, work began on a 10-h.p. car to be sold along with the new 17-h.p. model. Like its larger brother, the 10 h.p. had a four-cylinder engine, but it was built by the Nero Engine Co. (part of Riley), and had a capacity of 1096 c.c. This new model was due to make its debut at Olympia in 1914, retailing at around half the price of the 17 h.p., but the outbreak of war made this impossible.

In 1916 the Nero Engine Co. bought land in Foleshill and built bays of a new works to further help with the war effort. Subsequently, this site would become the main Riley works.

As soon as peace was declared, it was decided that the detachable-wheel production should cease, and that Riley (Coventry) Ltd would absorb the Nero Engine Co. The company then moved into the newer factory at Foleshill, abandoning the old works in St Nicholas Street, to build a final series of 17/30-h.p. cars.

A week before the first post-war Motor Show, Riley disclosed the details of their new models. It was at Olympia in 1919 that the 11 h.p. was initially shown. This car was the first Riley to bear the now famous 'V' shape in the radiator grille, and the equally famous Riley diamond. Again, a four-cylinder monobloc construction was used for the engine, but this time the capacity rose to 1.5 litres. This model gained much critical acclaim, and performed as well on the track and in trials as it had on the roads.

Following the Redwing model (so named because of its coachwork) came the famous Riley Nine. Designs for this model were completed in 1925, with the pretty 'Monaco' saloon bodywork first appearing in the summer of 1926 at Shelsley Walsh. It was well ahead of its time in terms of engine design, and this superb vehicle stayed in production until from 1927 to 1937.

The next milestone in the company's history was probably the introduction of the Brooklands Nine in 1927. With this car, Riley bridged the gap in the British market for the small sports car in a field dominated by Bugatti and other foreign marques. The Brooklands Nine had a shortened chassis and a slightly modified engine of 1.1 litres. The racing history of this vehicle, at least within its class, was impeccable, including numerous wins. Virtually all of these particular Nines were assembled at the famous Thomson & Taylor works, situated at the Brooklands track itself.

The White Riley pictured at a Riley Register meeting in Coventry in 1977

The first six-cylinder Riley appeared at the 1928 Motor Show in a body named the Stelvio. Rated at 14 h.p., this 1600-c.c. engine developed a maximum of 50 h.p. and was basically one and a half 9-h.p. four-cylinder engines.

By 1930, the company had made an incredible £1 million worth of sales, and by the end of the following year Riley (Coventry) Ltd had taken over the Riley Engine Co. and the Midland Motor Body Co. During the early 1930s several boat-building concerns were supplied with Riley Nine marine engines, while car sales continued to boom.

The 9- and 14-h.p. models maintained their success on the track, with both the road and racing versions undergoing many detail and body changes. After a long gap, the factory issued a totally new body-shape. The Kestrel was marketed in time for the 1933 trading season, along with another 9-h.p. vehicle – the Falcon – and the Lynx.

The 10.8-h.p. Riley was introduced in 1919 (this tourer dates from 1922)

One of the Brooklands Nine 1933 team cars pictured at a Silverstone race-meeting

1932 coach-built Riley Monaco

Raymond Mays had entered a modified and supercharged 160-b.h.p. Riley in the 1933 Brooklands August Bank Holiday meeting. Known as the 'White Riley', this superb vehicle was the forerunner of the famous ERA racing cars.

The Imp was intended to succeed the road version of the Brooklands Nine. Soon after the Imp was introduced, the MPH appeared. Both were extremely attractive, the MPH perhaps being slightly more beautiful, along the classic lines of the Alfa Monza. As if looking good wasn't enough, once again the Riley marque proved itself on the track, with more excellent results coming from the MPH model.

Just before the 1935 Motor Show it was disclosed that a Riley V8 engine was being developed. The new 2.2-litre V8 would power the six-light Kestrel and the Adelphi, the former being a most attractive car. Around the same time, the Merlin, a slightly inferior version of the Falcon, was introduced.

As a result of developments on the MPH chassis, the Sprite appeared out of the blue, sporting a completely different grille from the previous models. The engine was based on the new 1½-litre unit, first seen in late 1934.

A car that looked like a Riley, but was in fact a totally new make called the Autovia, made an appearance in 1937 at a Riley Motor Club meeting. The model was to be built with the 8/90, V8 Riley engine at Midland Road in Coventry, with Victor Riley as a director of the new business. The **Autovia** company was owned by the Riley family and Gordon Marshall. When Charles Van Eugen decided to leave the Riley camp late in 1934, he had been asked by Victor Riley to help manufacture this new luxury car, built on Riley principles. Only one prototype was in existence at the time, but Van Eugen, showing meticulous attention to detail, soon had a pre-production model ready. It is interesting to note that although Autovia supposedly had no links with Riley, initial development work was carried out at Durbar Avenue, before production was transferred to the Midland Road site.

The first Autovia car was completed towards the end of 1935. The V8 engines of 2849 c.c. developed around 99 b.h.p.; all of them were supplied by Riley. A preselector gearbox was fitted as standard, with the ZF manual gearbox following as an option later on.

The Autovia was quite a big car, with a wheelbase of 10' 9" and a track of 4' 8½". Even with these large dimensions, and despite its considerable weight, the vehicle was capable of over 90 m.p.h., while still returning a fuel consumption figure of around 18 m.p.g. The cost of the chassis was set at £685, with the elegant four-light sports body by Mulliner of Northampton being first priced at £975. The less popular limousine body, also by Mulliner, retailed at £995.

Autovia would eventually fade away in March 1938, with a total of only around forty cars ever having been built. It was later found that Riley Motors owned most of the company's shares, and this fine marque shared the fate of Autovia not long after.

In the mid-1930s a new Riley engine intended for the V8 chassis and known as the 'Big Four' was announced. The four-cylinder, 2½-litre engine would develop 85 b.h.p., and incorporated several novel features. The most attractive body offered on this chassis must surely have been the Big

A superb 1934 Riley MPH

One of the famous Autovia saloons

1937 Riley Kestrel-Sprite in New Zealand

1949 Riley R.M.A. 1½-litre saloon

Four 'Blue Streak' six-light Kestrel, which was initially priced at £415.

Owing to financial troubles, Riley made a last-ditch attempt at recovery by launching the Victor. Although the vehicle was fully equipped, the price was kept very low to try to attract as many customers as possible. Unfortunately, this failed to work, and the receiver was called in on 24 February 1938. Triumph negotiated the purchase of the company, but talks fell through.

Eventually Lord Nuffield stepped in and bought the business to add to his growing organization, marking the end of the 'real' Rileys. Like Daimler, Riley would continue in name only. Some of the vehicles, such as the RMF, were indeed built in the traditional Riley manner, but the later badge-engineered models did nothing for the excellent image that the company had created.

ERA have already been mentioned as a company that had links with Riley, since they originally used the six-cylinder MPH engines to power their racing cars. Healey too were connected with Riley, although well after the Nuffield takeover.

The Riley name finally died off quietly in 1969, having been applied to such BMC cars as the Farina 1½-litre saloons and even the Mini.

10

THE STANDARD-TRIUMPH GROUP

STANDARD BECAME ONE OF COVENTRY'S LARGEST COMPANIES. FOLLOWING THEIR PURCHASE OF TRIUMPH, THEY BECAME AN EVEN LARGER CONCERN. A LONG AND INTERESTING HISTORY WILL ALWAYS BE ASSOCIATED WITH THE MARQUE.

Standard, Much Park Street, Canley, 1903–1963
Triumph, Priory Street, Canley, 1923–1979

Reginald Maudslay established the Standard Motor Co. on 2 March 1903, in a small factory situated in Much Park Street. A large percentage of the capital needed to start up the business was given to Maudslay by his old employer, the designer of London's Tower Bridge, Sir John Wolfe Barry.

Maudslay's relations had taken his family name for their company some years beforehand, so 'Standard' was chosen instead, apparently to emphasize the firm's use of tried, tested and reliable components.

The first Standard car was a small single-cylinder machine with an underfloor engine. This was the work of Alex Craig, who had also designed for the Singer, Maudslay and Lea-Francis companies. A 12/15-h.p. twin was also available, with four-cylinder engines as an optional unit.

In 1904 the work-force consisted of only twenty men, but by 1906 this figure was five times greater. This rapid expansion led to the purchase of a new factory in Bishopsgate Green. The old buildings were used by the coach-building firm of Charlesworth Bodies, and later by Lea-Francis.

By 1906 Standard were offering the country's first inexpensive six-cylinder car. The vehicles had side valves, three-speed gearboxes and a shaft drive. Other Standard cars of the time included a 24/30-h.p., a 3.3-litre 20-h.p., and a larger 50-h.p. car, which sold for £850. It was around this time that Charles Friswell of London was chairman of the company. The appointment came about after he signed a

Reginald Maudslay, founder of the Standard Motor Co.

This 1907 Standard is thought to be the oldest car of the marque still in existence.

The shouldered radiator of the early Standards first carried the famous Union Jack badge in 1908. In the following year, a new 2.7-litre four-cylinder model was introduced. Rated at 14 h.p., it sold at £350. Other fours continued to be placed on the market, and the sixes were finally dropped from the range towards the end of 1912.

A large car of small proportions, the 9.5-h.p. SLS was announced in 1913. It featured a three-speed gearbox and worm drive, and all braking was applied to the rear wheels. This car was introduced at just £185. Two years later, electric lighting had become available for this baby of the range, and it was also fitted to the other two cars launched before the outbreak of the First World War – a 2.4 litre and a 3.3 litre, both being side-valve monobloc fours.

This astonishing amount of early success meant that Standard had become one of the largest companies in Coventry. During the war, Standard were given the contract to build RE8 biplanes, and this work was carried out in the new factory at Canley. The smaller operations, such as building the odd vehicle and shell-making, continued in the old factory. Standard now employed over 2000 people.

Just after the war, an enlarged, 1.3-litre version of the SLS was produced, and this soon became the model that would provide Standard with their bread and butter. In 1921 it grew once again, this time into the o.h.v., 11.6-h.p. SLO model. As with many of these early vintage Standards, there were no sides to the radiator shells.

By now the company had occupied the large factory at

contract to sell the whole output of six-cylinder cars through his showrooms, and lasted for around five years, until this arrangement came to an end. Friswell's shares were later sold to a Coventry solicitor and to Siegfried Bettmann, the founder of the Triumph company. Ironically, it was Bettmann who took over the chair from Friswell in 1911.

Six-cylinder models dominated the Standard range for quite a few years, and when the 'Twenty' was up-rated to a 4-litre car, sales continued at a steady rate. In one order alone, seventy of these models were shipped out to India.

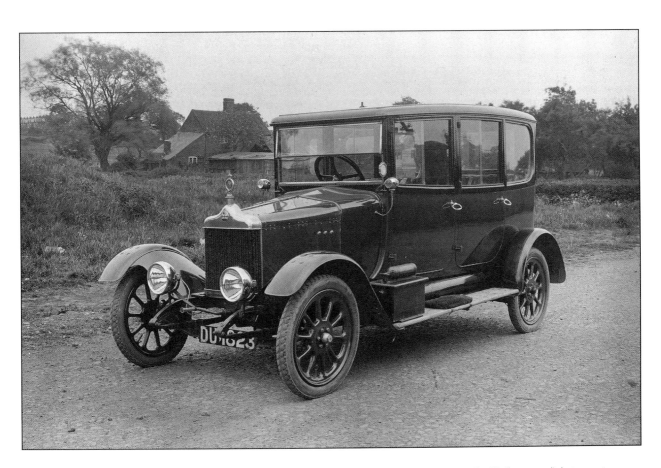

Prototype saloon based on the Standard SLS. By far the most popular body fitted to the SLS chassis was the 'Rhyl', a pretty little two-seater.

Canley for several years, but in 1922 a moving body-assembly track was installed, as well as a test circuit built around the outside of the works.

For the 1922 season, there was a short-lived o.h.v., 8-h.p. model, but the 13.9-h.p. SLO4 introduced shortly afterwards proved to be a far greater success. Still sporting an overhead-valve arrangement, and worm drive, the SLO4 had rigid side-curtains and could be bought for £375 in 1924. Standard radiators were now carrying the emblem of the Ninth Roman Legion. A staggering 10000 cars had been sold during 1924.

Front-wheel brakes were a standard feature on the 13.9-h.p. cars of 1926. In the following year, an unsuccessful 2.2-litre o.h.v. six-cylinder model was announced, but at least saloons could now be bought with sliding roofs.

Financial difficulties around 1928 led to the hurried introduction of the excellent 1155-c.c. worm-driven 'Nine'. It had a side-valve engine and fabric bodywork. Fortunately for the company, this car was an immediate success, and within a year many new versions were listed. They included a roomier, longer-wheelbase model, a sports two-seater (with either a standard or supercharged engine) and the first of the Avon Standard Specials – a low-built two-seater, styled by the Jensen brothers. The Avon, both in its original form and later as Beauvais-styled concepts on other Standard chassis, would stay in production for nearly a decade.

The year 1929 saw the introduction of a range of side-valve sixes with coil ignition and seven-bearing crankshafts. The new line would persist until 1940, but perhaps more important was the appointment of Captain J.P. Black as managing director. He was originally brought to the company from Hillman, and under his control, Standard would conquer the Depression with steadily increasing sales. Several other top engineers joined Standard from the Rootes Group around this time, providing useful experience in many different areas.

By 1931, magneto ignition, worm-driven back axles and the traditional radiator had all disappeared for good, and the current range comprised the roomy small saloon known as the Big Nine, which sold for under £200, and the low-priced sixes rated at 16 and 20 h.p. respectively.

The 1-litre Little Nine was employed by William Lyons as the basis for his 'SS2' car. Lyons' 1930 Swallow-bodied Standards had anticipated the new 1931 radiator, but his SS models were to use specially built Standard chassis and his own style of bodywork. Standard-built engines were to feature in all of Lyons' cars until around 1940, and continued in the four-cylinder Jaguars into 1948, although by then, Jaguar owned all the tooling for the power units, and so built them themselves.

The 1933 Standards were fitted with cruciform-braced frames, and gearboxes with a 'silent third'. The range was becoming complex: a couple of short-lived sixes of under 1.5 litres, the option of preselector gearboxes on some models and a long-wheelbase laundaulette, rated at 20 h.p.

Integral boots, synchromesh and free wheels all arrived in 1934, as did the company's new best seller – the well-equipped 1.3-litre 'Ten'. The sad news of the death of Reginald Maudslay, the company's founder, must have cast a

1930 Avon Standard Special (left) with a Standard Teignmouth. Note how low the Avon-bodied car is.

A delightful publicity shot of one of the early 'Flying Standards'

The prototype Standard V8. Although the car was not a great success, the grille features on all Standards for several years.

shadow on Standard's success, but Black soldiered on, and for the following year, there were six models; these included the sporting 10/12 h.p., which was basically a Ten with a larger, twin-carburettor, 1.6-litre 12-h.p. engine. Much the same range was offered for 1936, although the fastback Flying Standards did make their debut. The luggage accommodation and spare wheels were streamlined into the tails, with a choice of either 12-, 16-, or 20-h.p. engines.

By 1937 this new style was universal, and buyers had the option of four four-cylinder and two six-cylinder power units. The range went from the Nine, priced at £149, to the Twenty, at £299. A rapid and compact V8 also appeared. The 2.7-litre, 80-b.h.p. engine was mounted in a Twelve chassis. Unfortunately, the model wasn't the success it was expected to be, although it did attract the attention of Raymond Mays, who is thought to have built five 'Specials' based on the type. The grille would also be a feature of all Standards from 1938 to 1947, so it wasn't all bad news.

Railton based their 'Ten' on a Standard chassis, and Morgan had their own special 10-h.p. engine built at the factory, but these were just two of the many manufacturers that Standard supplied. By 1939 the company had become one of Coventry's two largest assemblers in their own right.

Just before war was declared, the 1-litre 'Eight', costing just £129, had taken over as the company's best seller. It was the first British small saloon with independent front suspension. A similar suspension layout could be found on the 'Super' versions of the Ten and the Twelve, but the Flying Standards of this year did not have the fastback styling.

There was a massive wartime output from Standard, and, along with Rootes, the company were to be one of the first firms in Coventry to welcome women recruits and put them through a formal training scheme. Over 1000 Mosquito fighter/bombers were produced, as well as Oxford Trainers, light vehicles, aircraft engines and literally thousands of components. All of this helped to earn Black a knighthood and give the factory a well-deserved £6 million modernization scheme.

Only the Eight, Twelve and Fourteen were continued after the war, the latter now being a Twelve chassis fitted with a 1.8-litre engine, but now the factory's products included Triumphs, Standard having managed to buy the company during the last year of the hostilities.

The first true post-war Standard was the Vanguard. This came in 1947, and had a 2.1-litre o.h.v. four-cylinder engine, full-width six-seater bodywork, hydraulic braking and a three-speed gearbox with a column selector. At just under £550, it should have been a very popular car indeed, though it was some time before it became readily available on the home market. The Vanguard continued to be the only Standard model listed between 1949 and 1953.

By now, Imperia were building Standard cars under licence in Belgium, and because of the Government export drive, the Vanguard was assembled in ten more countries also. The Vanguard engine was successfully applied to the bigger Triumphs of the time, as well as Ferguson tractors, the first Plus-Four Morgan and, in 2-litre form, the excellent Triumph TR series.

The Vanguard underwent several changes in its long life.

Sir John Black with one of the very first Standard Vanguards

Overdrive was made available as an option in 1950, and the body was redesigned in 1953, 1956 and 1959. For 1954/55, a diesel version was marketed, and a luxury 'Sportsman' version with a 90-b.h.p. engine and traditional grille also made an appearance in 1957. This model proved to be too expensive, though, and was discontinued shortly afterwards. Automatic transmission was introduced towards the end of the Vanguard run, and the model was finally laid to rest in 1961.

A small and very basic 803-c.c. car was announced late in 1953, followed almost immediately by a plusher example with a 948-c.c. engine. This model, the Ten, sold for just over £580. These were the first Standards to feature a monocoque body, but even the addition of the luxury 'Pennant' model in 1957 failed to stir up much enthusiasm for the type, although Fairthorpe employed the engine for their cars, and it later formed the basis for the Triumph Herald unit.

From 1951, Standard built the Rolls-Royce Avon jet engine under licence — proof, if it were ever needed, that Standard had a very skilled work-force. At the beginning of 1954, a boardroom revolution resulted in the departure of Sir John Black. His dictatorial leadership had become a little too much for his colleagues to bear, and so it was that his long-time assistant, Alick Dick, took over as the new managing director.

Standard had owned the Banner Lane factory for many years. It had been a Shadow Factory during the war, and several interesting stories can be told about it: first, there were plans to build a four-wheel-drive vehicle for farmers there, then there was talk of a merger with Willys-Overland to produce the famous Jeep in Coventry, but in the end Standard decided to manufacture Harry Ferguson tractors instead. This was in 1946, but in 1959 Standard sold the business to the Canadian firm of Massey Harris for £12

1949 Ferguson 20 tractor

Standard Vanguard Vignale

million. It was with the proceeds of this sale that the company managed to acquire the Tile Hill-based Fisher & Ludlow body-making plant, Beans Industries, Alford & Adler, Hall Engineering (Holdings) Ltd and Mulliner's of Birmingham.

By now, Standard's financial situation was weakening. The high development costs of the Herald (which would eventually make its debut as a Triumph!) did not help matters. Several possible mergers had been considered, including one with Rover. Even an attempt to stay afloat by entering the light-commercial market with the Atlas range of vehicles was foiled. Production of the small Standards ended, and the company was taken over by Leyland Motors in 1961. Alick Dick was asked to resign, and Stanley Markland moved down from Liverpool and was appointed the new managing director.

The Ensign had originally been a 1.6-litre car loosely based on the Vanguard, but this model was revived in 1962 and give a larger 2.1-litre engine which developed around 75 b.h.p. However, after the Leyland takeover, Standard became the poor relation, and the company tended to concentrate on the Triumph range.

About two years after Markland took up his position at the head of Standard-Triumph, he decided to take early retirement. His successor was Donald Stokes, who would look after Leyland Trucks at the same time. Within two years of Stokes' arrival, losses turned into healthy profits, allowing

the company to buy up Rover, a move that subsequently created British Leyland. The last car to be marketed under the Standard marque was the Vanguard-based Ensign De Luxe. The final batch of these rolled out of the factory in the summer of 1963, although the last of the commercials was not sold until 1965. Atlas engines and cabs persisted for a further three years, whilst Scammell were still using them.

As mentioned earlier in this chapter, Standard continued to build **Triumph** vehicles, having acquired the company during the Second World War. With Triumph, Sir John Black would try to take trade away from SS Cars, who by now had rather a large chunk of the sports-car market.

This marque started life as the Triumph Cycle Co., which was founded by Siegfried Bettmann, along with his partner Mauritz Schulte. Bettmann was a German Jew who had come to England in 1884 at the age of twenty-one. He took on several agencies in the London area, and eventually started to export cycles under the name of Triumph. Originally, these were built for him in Birmingham, but in 1887 he came to Coventry to set up his own factory.

Harvey DuCros (of Dunlop fame) injected a large amount of cash into the business in 1895, and it was then that things really took off. Just two years later, the Triumph Cycle Co. went public, with experimental motorcycles being built in 1898. Surprisingly, motorcycle production did not begin until 1902, but it was only a further three years before

Triumph were building their own engines to power them.

As noted earlier, Siegfried Bettmann became chairman of the Standard Motor Co. in 1911, but it is interesting to note that he also held the office of Lord Mayor of Coventry in 1913.

Although a tricar was built in 1903, it wasn't until twenty years later that the company's first four-wheeler was built: a 1.4-litre four-cylinder car, rated at 10/20 h.p. The power from this Ricardo-designed engine was driven through a four-speed gearbox, and the vehicle sold for £430. At this stage, production was undertaken in the old Dawson works.

In 1924 a new 1.9-litre model, known as the 13/30, was introduced, but neither this car, nor its 15-h.p. successor, made much of an impression, despite the fact that the former was the first British car to feature Lockheed contracting-type hydraulic brakes. It was the 832-c.c. 'Super Seven' of 1927 that really got things moving for Triumph as a car manufacturer. With its unit gearbox, hydraulic brakes and worm final drive, it sold well both at home and abroad, in direct competition with the Austin Seven. A supercharged sports version was also produced in the following two years, but it was the manufacture of small, high-quality family saloons that would dominate the factory's output until around 1934. About 17000 Super Sevens were built; in contrast, the total number of all previous models produced was around 2000!

Ribbon-type radiators were introduced in 1930, and in the following year, a 1.2-litre, small six-cylinder car, the Scorpion,

made its debut. It was basically a Super Seven with two extra cylinders and lower gearing. By this time, the Depression was biting hard. It was decided to sell the cycle business to Coventry Bicycles, and the motorcycle section nearly went too.

Coventry Climax inlet-over-exhaust engines were first used in 1932, in the Triumph Super Nine. Saloons had pillarless doors and four-speed gearboxes. The larger 1933 models were joined by the 1.1-litre 'Ten' during the season, and this was introduced at £225.

Although these family models were still being built in 1934, the company's emphasis now shifted towards sporting cars. The Gloria was available with either a 1.1-litre four-cylinder, or a 1.5-litre six-cylinder engine. A cruciform-braced chassis was used, as were free wheels, and in open form the car could quite easily exceed 70 m.p.h.

It is unfortunate that nothing ever came of Triumph's 2-litre double-o.h.c. supercharged straight-eight, although, because it was priced at £1225, it is hardly any wonder! This was one of Donald Healey's projects, and the engine was almost a replica of the classic Alfa Romeo 8C unit. It is thought that only three prototypes were ever built. Much more successful was the 1935 Gloria-Vitesse, especially in 2-litre, six-cylinder guise. A metallic paint finish was available on this model, and the saloons were fitted with windscreen-washers as standard. It was during 1935 that Triumph acquired the old White & Poppe works, providing valuable extra capacity.

Triumph Super Seven

A beautiful Triumph Gloria-Vitesse. This 1934 example belongs to the Patrick Collection.

In 1936 the car and motorcycle businesses went their separate ways. Motorcycle production stayed in the original Priory Street works until 1940, when it was destroyed by heavy bombing. Post-war machines were built in nearby Meriden, where they continued to be produced until the mid 1980s.

From 1937, the cars became heavier, and Triumph-built o.h.v. engines supplanted the Coventry Climax units. The models ranged from the 1½-litre Gloria saloon right up to the 1.8-litre four-cylinder and 2-litre six-cylinder Dolomites. Triumph now had its own excellent coach-building department, although outside contracts were still being awarded to the likes of Tickford and Cross & Ellis. Donald Healey was the company's technical director, and thanks to him, Triumph gained a number of early competition successes.

The Dolomites were not only well equipped but particularly handsome, winning many *concour d'élégance* awards. From the summer of 1938, only Dolomite models were listed. A conventionally styled 12-h.p. sports saloon joined the ranks in 1939, but only fifty were built before Triumph went into receivership in June of the same year.

After the war had ended, cars were produced by Standard, Triumph vehicles being built alongside Standard ones at Canley. Sir John Black had bought the remains of the Priory Street factory in 1944, the sale including the rights to the Triumph name. The old works were soon sold off, and a subsidiary of Standard – the Triumph Motor Co. (1945) Ltd – was formed.

The new 1800 was fitted with the same four-cylinder engine that powered the Jaguars of the time, and it had Girling brakes and a four-speed gearbox with a column change. Both the roadster and the saloon were traditionally styled, and sold at £799 and £831 respectively. The saloon version featured the 'razor-edge' body style favoured by the specialist coach-builders of the late thirties. This model later became known as the Renown. By 1949, the Standard

The superb straight-eight-engined Triumph Dolomite, pictured here with its designer, Donald Healey. 'ADU 4' was the first Dolomite to run.

1959 Triumph TR3A

Once the Herald was introduced, the Standard-Triumph group took a new interest in competition. This is the car driven by Corbishly on the Monte-Carlo Rally.

A fine example of a Triumph 1800 roadster, a model suddenly made popular by a certain television series.

Vanguard engine of 2.1 litres had been adopted, and in the following year the Mayflower, a small two-door saloon, appeared. This model, fitted with a 10-h.p. side-valve engine, remained in production for about three years.

It was in 1953 that the first of the famous TR line of cars made its debut. An advanced 1950 design (code-named the TRX) that became a casualty of the Korean War should have been the first model, but it was the TR2 which made it on to the market. Fitted with the 2-litre development of the Vanguard engine, it developed 90 b.h.p. This, combined with its light weight, allowed the vehicle to reach speeds in excess of 100 m.p.h., while remaining capable of returning 25 m.p.g. in normal usage. Other features included independent coil-and-wishbone front suspension, Lockheed brakes and a hypoid final drive. The TR2 became very popular in the U.S.A., and performed well in competition.

The TR2 power unit was adopted by Swallow Doretti, Morgan, Peerless and Warwick cars. Incidentally, the Swallow Doretti could well have been one of the cars described in this book, had Sir John Black got his own way. He was being driven in one by Ken Richardson when they had an accident outside the Banner Lane gates, and negotiations to purchase

the company never went any further. Triumph's next model was the TR3, which had acquired front disc brakes by 1956.

The 2.1-litre razor-edged Renown saloon was gradually discontinued, until, by 1955, it was the TR that had become the staple Triumph product. That is, until mid-way through 1959, when the Herald saloon put in an appearance. This Michelotti-styled vehicle used a development of the old 948-c.c. Standard Ten engine, and it featured a collapsible steering column, and all-round independent suspension – the first small British family saloon to be so equipped. Either a 38-b.h.p. single-carburettor or a 50-b.h.p. twin-carburettor engine could be specified, and prices started at just £702. This model didn't really prosper until Leyland took over the group in 1961, when a more powerful version was marketed. By 1963, front disc brakes were a standard fitment, as was a sunshine roof. A 1.6-litre six-cylinder derivative, the Vitesse, was announced in 1962, and another Herald development, a two-seater sports car known as the Spitfire, was introduced for the 1963 season.

These were interesting times for the 'competition department' at Banner Lane also. The 1959 Le Mans race had seen TR3As compete with 'Sabrina' engines, a

Sprucer performance with more comfortable ride.

The new Triumph TR4A goes independent all round and all civilised inside

We have given the new TR4A a certain type of independent rear suspension because it has the best inherent anti-roll characteristics. We chose the trailing-arm type (using coil springs and piston dampers) for its utter simplicity and reliability. The gain? Faster, tighter cornering, improved road-holding, and a smoother ride.

THE CIVILISED TOUCH

Second biggest change is the *convertible hood*. You just unclip it and fold it right back into the body. It comes up just as fast. We have also reshaped the bucket seats and covered them in supple Ambla.

The facia panel now boasts walnut veneer. Liberal padding improves safety and appearance of the facia surround, door waist rails and sun visors. There's door-to-door carpeting.

FAIR WARNING

On a car this fast you need early-warning equipment. There are long-range horns under the bonnet. A head-lamp flasher on the steering column. And new indicator repeaters on the wings. Two-speed windscreen wipers as well.

Try it. Visit your local Standard-Triumph dealer. He'll show you the paces of the new TR4A. It takes 20 minutes of your time and a willingness to appreciate progress in sports motoring.

Ex-works prices inc. p.t.
TR4A Soft Top Model £968.4.7
Hard Top Model £1,010.10.5

STANDARD TRIUMPH

A member of the Leyland Motor Corporation

lightweight twin-cam unit, but unfortunately the three works cars all failed to finish. In the following year, though, the same engine was used in the TRS racer. With its bodywork based on the Michelotti 'Zoom' project, this model was to be the starting-point for the next stage of the TR run. Although not particularly successful, the TRS remains an important car in the history of Triumph.

The TR4 came in 1962. It featured restyled bodywork, a 2.1-litre engine, rack-and-pinion steering and an all-synchromesh gearbox. When the model gained independent rear suspension in 1965, it was designated the TR4A. The TR4 range was the first of the classic line to be approved by the new Leyland management team, but it was still very much in keeping with traditional TR values.

The lovely Triumph 2000 was introduced in 1964. The 2-litre, six-cylinder engine it was fitted with developed a healthy 90 b.h.p. and this model proved to be a great success, staying in production in various forms until 1977. A front-wheel-drive car was announced in 1966. This model, known simply as the 1300, had front disc brakes and an all-round independent suspension. This small saloon would also continue to be developed and built for many years to come.

The 2-litre engine was used in the 1967 MY Vitesses, as well as in the new GT6, a hard-top coupé based on the Spitfire. The TR5 was introduced in the following year, with a new 2½-litre fuel-injected engine, and the 1300 became available in the more powerful TC form.

For 1969, the range was revised. Wishbone rear suspension was adopted on the Vitesse and GT6, and a de-tuned version of the newly introduced TR6 engine was dropped into the Triumph 2000 body-shell, making a new and more expensive model, called the 2.5 PI. Although at this time Triumph were building four-cylinder o.h.c. engines for SAAB, their own four-cylinder cars continued to be fitted with the old o.h.v. units.

A new luxury 2+2 sports car made its debut in 1970. Named the Stag, it was powered by a superb 3-litre double-o.h.c. V8 engine, which developed around 145 b.h.p. Power-assisted steering was fitted as standard, with automatic transmission being listed as an option. The beautiful coachwork concealed a semi-convertible design feature with a built-in roll-bar.

The Toledo saloon replaced the Herald in 1971. It was a combination of the Herald's running gear and the body of the 1300. A more powerful 1500 soon superseded this new model, with the luxury Dolomite coming at the beginning of 1972. This followed the Toledo lines, but was fitted with an overhead-camshaft engine of 1.85 litres.

All front-wheel-drive saloons were finally dropped from the range in 1974, the TR6 following one year later. In 1977, both the Stag and the six-cylinder saloons (now sporting twin carburettors only) were also deleted. By now, several changes had affected the company; up until 1975, the cars had kept their Triumph identity, but from then on, they would be classed as just another Leyland car. Another change came in 1978. British Leyland decided to make the company part of the specialist group of Jaguar-Rover-Triumph Ltd, but this arrangement lasted only a couple of years. However, it did cost Triumph any future large saloons, as they would go on to be badged as Rovers.

The Spitfire had been fitted with a 1½-litre engine since 1975. In this form, it did manage to continue into 1980. The Dolomite and Toledo ranges had been rationalized in 1976, but the surviving types also made it into the eighties – just. This line of cars was headed by the delightful Dolomite Sprint, with its 2-litre, 16-valve single-o.h.c. engine, which developed over 125 b.h.p.

In 1975, the TR6 was replaced by the wedge-shaped TR7. It used the Dolomite Sprint power unit in a unitary hull, all-coil springing, rack-and-pinion steering and power-assisted brakes – discs to the front. In 1977 the original four-speed gearbox was replaced by a Rover five-speed one, but it wasn't until two years later that the first convertible mdoels appeared. By the end of 1979, production of the TR7 had been moved to Solihull. There was also a U.S.A.-only car, dubbed the TR8, that was powered by the Rover 3½-litre V8 engine – surely one of the most desirable later Triumphs. During the autumn of 1981, Triumph's last sports cars left the factory, leaving only the Acclaim to keep the marque alive. Even this very nearly didn't happen, as the car was originally going to be badged as an MG model.

The Acclaim was a joint venture between Triumph and Honda of Japan. Talks between the two companies had begun as far back as 1979, but this new front-wheel-drive vehicle didn't appear until the 1982 sales season. This collaboration with Honda saved British Leyland a massive amount of development costs. With several trim options and

Concours-winning 1973 Triumph Stag

Two historic Triumphs from recent years. The 1977 2500TC (right) was the last of its type to be used by the Coventry Police Force. Next to it is a 1973 Dolomite Sprint, the actual car shown at Zurich and Earls Court. It was later used as a factory demonstration model.

a 1.3-litre power unit, the Acclaim was aimed straight at the popular small family car market. Later on, production of the Acclaim was moved to Oxford. The Acclaim was to be a short-lived car, however, and the Triumph marque came to a sudden and untimely end, its successor being the 1984 Rover 200 series.

The old Standard site at Canley is now occupied by Austin-Rover, or the Rover Group, to be exact. This has been the case since 1980, although the failure of British Leyland led not only to the loss of car production at Canley, but also to the closure of the old Morris Engines works at Courthouse Green.

The last car to bear the Triumph name: the Acclaim

11

ROOTES AND AFTER

THE LONG AND EVENTFUL HISTORY OF THE ROOTES
BROTHERS AND THEIR EMPIRE IS A FASCINATING ONE,
INVOLVING MANY ESTABLISHED COVENTRY COMPANIES.

Humber, *Humber Road, 1896–1968*
Hillman-Coatalen, *Hood Street, 1907–1910*
Hillman, *Humber Road, 1910–1976*
Commer/Karrier, *Humber Road, 1925–1968*
Sunbeam-Talbot, *Ryton, 1946–1954*
Chrysler U.K., *Humber Road, Ryton, 1968–1978*
Talbot, *Ryton, 1978–1979*
Peugeot-Talbot, *Ryton, 1979–*

Also included:
Singer, *Canterbury Street, 1900–1970*
Clément, *Parkside, 1908–1914*
Calcott, *Far Gosford Street, 1913–1926*
Coventry-Premier, *Read Street, 1913–1923*

Lord Rootes (left), with Cary Grant and an Imp

Contrary to popular belief, the Rootes family were not always rich and powerful; indeed, their beginnings were fairly humble. It was William Rootes Senior who first entered the industry, at the turn of the century, by setting up his own cycle repair business in Kent. It was here, just after the First World War, that his two sons, William and Reginald, began to develop the retail motor trade in which their father had become involved during the Edwardian period.

The two brothers had skills which complemented each other, and they became extremely successful, establishing a large chain of dealerships in a very short space of time. During the early 1920s their headquarters were situated in London's Long Acre, and by 1926 they had acquired a brand new building in Piccadilly called Devonshire House. They were fast becoming the country's largest and most powerful car distributors. Incredible though it may seem, William was looking to expand still further by becoming directly involved with the manufacturers.

After unsuccessful attempts to acquire Clyno and Standard, the big chance for Rootes came in 1928, when the Coventry firms of Humber, Hillman and the commercial-vehicle builders Commer were forced to merge, mainly due to the domination of Morris and Austin during this time. Initially, Rootes only looked after the export activities of the newly formed partnership, but by the following year William and Reginald were effectively the company policy-makers. The range of cars was immediately rationalized. Just before the war, two Hillmans, five Humbers and four Sunbeam-Talbots were all produced from only two engine families, two gearbox and axle families, three basic chassis and three standard body-styles. Both Spencer Wilks and John Black decided to leave Hillman at this stage. However, they helped turn the fortunes of two other Coventry marques: Rover and Standard.

Rootes Ltd had been buying shares in Humber whenever they became available, and by 1931, they owned 60 per cent of the company. A management takeover came in June of

Devonshire House in London, headquarters of the Rootes Empire

the following year, and the Rootes Group was officially founded. The group became well respected in the years leading up to the Second World War, and it was because of this that the factory at Ryton came about. Its original purpose was to be a shadow factory for the manufacture of aero-engines. Once the hostilities ceased, though, Ryton was to become the centre of all Rootes activities, having miraculously escaped the worst of the bombing.

In the autumn of 1938, a new marque was launched by Rootes: Sunbeam-Talbot. Sunbeam and Talbot had been acquired a few years earlier after the Sunbeam–Talbot–Darracq (STD) combine went bankrupt, and although these new cars were really just high-performance versions of Humbers and Hillmans, they would develop a following of their own, mainly due to their successes in motor sport – rallying in particular. By now, the Rootes Group was one of the largest concerns in the motor industry as a whole.

After the war, Rootes continued to expand, and bought up yet another old Coventry company in 1956. This time it

Ryton just after the Second World War

was Singer who became just one more badge that the group could engineer.

Like all good things, the group eventually came to an end. Some bad luck and a few bad decisions finally led to the downfall of the empire. Lord Rootes (Sir William was ennobled in 1959) died at the end of 1964. Some say that it was overwork that killed him. At around the same time, control of the group was gained by Chrysler, although the Rootes name survived until 1968, after which 'Chrysler U.K.' was adopted.

The story doesn't quite end here, of course, but this is an ideal opportunity to introduce the individual companies that made up the Rootes Group.

Humber

Thomas Humber's bicycle firm was established in 1869 in the small village of Beeston, in Nottinghamshire. The business grew steadily, and gained new works at both Coventry and Wolverhampton in around 1887, a year after it became a limited company. An American branch was even set up in 1894. The Coventry factory was a large block of premises, the main building being four storeys high, and extending 150 feet in depth. Briefly it became part of H.J. Lawson's intended automobile empire, and as such was responsible for the production of the ill-fated Pennington tricars. Car manufacture began with an experimental front-wheel-drive model, although at the time, motor tricycles and quadricycles were being produced in large numbers. These led to a range of three-wheeled forecars, sold under the name of Coventry Bollée, which stayed in production until 1905. Even the devastating fire at the factory in 1896 didn't deter the management; they just set up shop in the Motor Mills for a while, until things could get back to normal.

Very little came of Humber's first voiturette with a two-speed gear, but their more conventional 1901 offering, with 4½-h.p. De Dion engine and transmission, proved more successful. Unique at the time was Humber's single-spoked steering-wheel — nearly half a century before Citroën used them.

A 12-h.p. four-cylinder car made its debut in 1902, to be followed by some more ambitious vehicles in 1903: a 20-h.p. four, and a three-cylinder version with mechanically operated inlet valves. The 5-h.p. Humberette, with its De Dion-based 613-c.c. engine, was to be Britain's first successful light car. All of these vehicles were shaft-driven, as Humber tried to avoid chains.

Until 1908, two separate lines of cars were built under the Humber name. There were the Coventry-built cars, and there were those built in Beeston, the latter being the more expensive. In 1905, a small 'four' rated at 8/10-h.p. appeared. It was to be developed in the following year into a 10/12-h.p. Coventry-Humber. This model sold at £315, whereas the Beeston offering, a 3½-litre T-head four-cylinder car, retailed at £472. The 1907 Beeston models sported a new 6.3-litre engine capacity.

The chief designer at Humber since 1901 had been Louis Coatalen (a name which will appear on many occasions!), but he left in 1908 to join Hillman. Nevertheless, the line-up of models available just before he left was quite extensive. It

1934 12-h.p. Humber

Thomas Humber

ranged from the 1½-litre 8-h.p. vertical twin, aimed at the light-car market, right through to the large 5½-litre six-cylinder model, also Coventry-built, and selling for the modest sum of £450.

By now, Humber had acquired the old factory that used to belong to Bayliss, Thomas & Co., as well as the Progress Cycle Works. The new 22½-acre Stoke site was also being made ready at this time, in what is now known as Humber Road. It had taken nearly two years to build the new plant, but as soon as the last of the machines was installed in 1908, this massive factory made the other, smaller units redundant, and they were all closed down. However, Humber and Daimler continued to be amongst the largest employers in the British engineering industry.

The first Humber car built in Coventry: the 5-h.p. Humberette

A gathering outside the Humber works

The Beeston factory was forced to close in 1908, but the T-headed cars, all of which were equipped with four-speed gearboxes by 1911, continued to be built in Coventry. In 1912 the new L-headed models made their debut, including an 11-h.p. sporting a 1.7-litre monobloc engine, and a cyclecar (Humber were one of the few major manufacturers to enter this field) with a 998-c.c. air-cooled engine. This little machine, Humber's second Humberette, continued to be built until the outbreak of the First World War.

By 1913, Humber, along with Rover, Swift and Singer were producing an incredible 75 per cent of Coventry's car output. To put this into perspective, at that time, Coventry produced around a third of all the cars built in the United Kingdom.

Humber had supported the Tourist Trophy races right from the beginning, and for the 1914 race, a team of cars with 3.3-litre twin-o.h.c. engines was prepared. After the war, however, the company would concentrate on building good solid family cars, and they were noted for their excellent craftsmanship and high standard of equipment.

During the war, good use was made of the aeroplane department. In charge of this side of the Humber business was Captain Lovelace, who, along with the Frenchman Le Blon, saw one of their machines successfully complete the first air-mail run to India. The department had been formed in 1910, and built around twenty-five aircraft a week, mostly Avros. (*Further details in Appendix VIII.*)

Although car production had been stopped in 1916,

motorcycles continued to be built throughout the war. In fact, Humber motorcycles were still rolling out of the factory as late as 1930. Bicycles also continued to be made until 1932, when Raleigh purchased the rights.

The first post-war offerings were very much revivals of the pre-war models, the Ten and the Fourteen, although the latter was increased to 15.9 h.p. Side-valve engines were used until 1923, when they were replaced by inlet-over-exhaust layouts. It was also in this year that the small 8/18 model appeared. This sold for only £275. Surprisingly, front-wheel brakes were not yet fitted in some models, apparently

1923 Humber Chummy

This 1935 Humber Snipe is fairly typical of the period. Various bodies were available on the Snipe chassis.

because J.A. Cole, who was managing director at the time, distrusted them!

The company did not explore the commercial-vehicle market until 1925, when they bought **Commer** (Commercial Cars Ltd) of Luton. Because of the slump in the trade at this time, the price was very low. Three years later, they bought the **Hillman** outfit as well.

Humber managed to sell over 4000 vehicles in 1927. This was mainly due to the 1056-c.c. 9/20, the superb 2-litre 14/40 and the new 20/55 h.p., the company's first six-cylinder car for many years.

As mentioned earlier, the Rootes brothers had been buying all the Humber shares they could get their hands on, and this had given them a certain amount of control over the Humber-Hillman business. In mid-1932 they would take over the management of the company.

All the Humbers were restyled in 1929, and not long afterwards the effect of the Rootes influence was seen in the new line of six-cylinder cars: a 2.1-litre 16/50 and the 3½-litre Snipe. The Snipe's long-chassis counterpart was to be known as the Pullman. The master coach-builders of Thrupp & Maberly, who had become part of the empire some years earlier, were responsible for providing suitable bodies for this majestic vehicle. The 9-h.p. Humbers were deleted from the range, and from now on, most of the company's products would be larger family cars, aimed at the top end of the market. There is always one exception to the rule, and in 1933, a smaller car, the Twelve, powered by a 1.7-litre

engine, appeared. The engine was to form the basis for the long-stroke Rootes engines that continued in production through to 1966.

One important car in the Rootes history that failed to reach production was the 1936 Olympia Motor Show car. This luxury model used a Humber chassis, was badged as a Sunbeam and sported an eight-cylinder Roesch-Talbot engine. Two reasons have been given to explain why it never appeared again: one is that the chassis performed badly, and the other is Edward VIII's abdication. However unlikely the latter reason may seem, it could in fact be quite true, as the

The Humber Pullman was used by several Government departments as well as being employed for mayoral and royal duties all round the world. The example shown here is a 1950 Mark III.

1962 Series 4 Humber Super Snipe. The first of the monocoque-constructed series were seen in 1957, but the Hawk, Super Snipe and Imperial were phased out after the takeover by Chrysler in 1967. The luxury interiors featured the great British 'leather-and-walnut' tradition.

King was a great supporter of the marque; also, as the car was priced at £1500, he was probably the only person able to afford it!

By 1938, only six-cylinder models were being built. The largest of these cars now had a 4.1-litre engine, and all had been equipped with transverse independent front suspension a couple of years earlier. Hydraulic brakes became a standard fitment on the 16- and 21-h.p. versions in 1939, and they were also to be found on the new Super Snipe, a car that employed the 4.1-litre engine, mounted in a smaller chassis.

During the Second World War, Snipe-based vehicles served the Allied forces with great distinction. Viscount Montgomery used two famous cars: 'Old Faithful' was used for the desert campaign, while the 'Victory Car' was used in Europe. The latter is on permanent display in the Museum of British Road Transport in Coventry. Very many armoured and utility vehicles would also pass through the gates before the war finally came to an end.

The pre-war range was carried over, more or less unaltered, once the hostilities ceased. A new four-cylinder model, the 1.9-litre side-valve Hawk, was added, though, and this was based on the Hillman Fourteen of around 1940. Styling was slightly revised for the 1949 season, and a Super Snipe managed to take second place in the 1950 Monte Carlo Rally. This at least served to remind the public of the marque's pedigree.

The range developed at a steady pace – overhead valves, optional automatic transmission on the Super Snipes and unitary construction. The Hawk was redesigned in 1957, as

was the Super Snipe two years later, but this last vehicle re-emerged as an altogether smaller 2.6-litre car. It was soon replaced by a 3-litre development car which featured front disc brakes. The 1962 models would be fitted with a four-headlamp system.

A new small luxury Humber, based on the Hillman Super Minx, made its first appearance in 1964. This car was to be known as the Sceptre. During 1967 all of the big Humbers, including the Imperial, were discontinued due to rationalization by Chrysler. In theory, they were replaced by Australian-built Plymouth vehicles. Unfortunately, the only Humber offered since 1968 has been the prestige version of the Hillman Hunter, the 1.7-litre Sceptre, but the Humber will still go down in history as one of the world's finest cars.

1974 'Arrow'-type Humber Sceptre, the last car to bear the Humber name

Hillman

William Hillman was born in 1849, and began his career with the Coventry Machinists Co. In the early 1870s he founded the Hillman & Herbert Cycle Co. with his partner, W.H. Herbert. This firm later became known as the Premier Cycle Co., and Hillman was also responsible for setting up a German branch at Nuremberg.

To say that the Hillman car business originated in Hood Street is not strictly true, as the very first vehicles were built in the grounds of Hillman's home, Abingdon House. The earliest vehicles carried not only the Hillman name, but also that of their designer, Louis Coatalen. These Hillman-Coatalen cars were built on a very small scale, though there were some outstanding examples, due to William Hillman's passion for motor sport. By 1906, his interests in the Automachinery and New Premier companies had provided him with enough capital to build a car capable of winning the 1907 Tourist Trophy Race. A 25-h.p. four-cylinder model was built by Coatalen, who was recruited from Humber. In the following year's event, two cars were entered, but both the 6.4-litre cars failed to produce the desired results.

The large 6.4-litre four was joined by a 9.7-litre six, both with separately cast cylinders and side-valves, and both stayed in production right up until the outbreak of the First World War, even though hardly any sixes were sold. A smaller Hillman-Coatalen of 'only' 2.3 litres appeared in 1908, around the same time that the traditional Hillman radiator shape made its debut. This was to be a feature of the marque until around 1930.

Coatalen married one of Hillman's daughters, but in 1909 sold his share of the company back to his father-in-law. He then moved on to Sunbeam, and it is probably for this reason that Hillman eventually became associated more with family cars than with the sportier machines the firm was founded to produce in the first place.

In 1910 the name of the company was changed to the Hillman Motor Car Co. Ltd, and one of the first things it tried to do was to market a small taxi, but without much success. Two other fairly unsuccessful models were built in the immediate pre-war period: a 1.8-litre two-cylinder in 1913, and a two-litre six in the following year.

The A.J. Dawson-designed 9-h.p. model, with a 1357-c.c. monobloc four-cylinder engine, proved to be a good seller at only £200, and was updated after the war. Dawson went on to build cars under his own name at a later date but had already done enough to save the Hillman marque from an early death. By 1925, a 1.6-litre engine was the standard power unit for the model, and a sports version had also been marketed. It had a V-radiator, outside exhausts and polished aluminium bodywork. During the early twenties, it was raced quite regularly in home events.

John Black (also Hillman's son-in-law) was Dawson's successor, and he would stay with the company until 1930, when he joined Standard (see Chapter 10). The 11-h.p. 'Peace' model was in production early in 1919, and was offered with either two- or four-seater touring bodywork, or as a two-seater drop-head coupé. Even though the company could ill afford it, they still had a small competition department right up until Hillman's death in 1921. The works

William Hillman

A 1907 Hillman, driven by its designer, Louis Coatalen

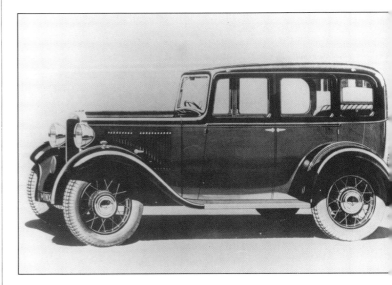

1931 Hillman Minx saloon

car came a creditable seventh in the 1921 Brooklands 200 Mile Race.

The Hillman range for 1923 to 1925 came with drop-head bodywork and winding windows. In the following year, a conventional side-valve Fourteen with a four-speed gearbox and magneto ignition was the only model offered by the company. Production of this particular vehicle was stepped up considerably after the merger with Humber in 1928. A companion for the Fourteen was built, though the Vortic, a 2.6-litre straight-eight, was never a real favourite with the buying public after some problems regarding big-end failure. None the less, it was still good enough to be the best-selling British straight-eight of all time.

Captain J.S. Irving, designer of Seagrave's 'Golden Arrow' Land Speed Record car, designed his first Hillman around 1928. Despite Irving's obvious skill, the 'Wizard', as it was known, was a bit of a flop. Even an attempt to prove the car by taking it and a caravan on the Monte Carlo Rally route failed to increase sales. Thankfully, Irving's next project was much more of a success.

Following the Rootes takeover, Hillman moved into the mass-production class with their cheap but excellent 1932 1.2-litre Minx. The Minx was progressively developed over the next few years, and the definitive version, the underslung Aero Minx sports model of 1933, became the basis for the Talbot and Sunbeam-Talbot Tens. There was even a luxury Humber Ten, also based on the Minx, though this was only ever built for the New Zealand market.

To complement the Minx-based models, there were also some six-cylinder side-valve cars, and these would eventually come equipped with a transverse independent front suspension. Another 1.9-litre Fourteen had superseded the type by 1940. The model was sold with hydraulic brakes – something not added to the Minx until the Phase II versions of late 1947 – and unit construction was used for the first time within the group.

The post-war Minxes continued to be the style leaders of mechanically conventional cars. The 1949 models had full-width five/six-seater bodywork, and there was a more powerful engine for 1950. A hard-top coupé version, known as the Californian, was introduced three years later. It is

This Hillman Imp is a former works rally car. It came second in the 1965 Tulip Rally, won the team prize in the 1967 Scottish Rally, and is still rallied today.

interesting to note that between 1953 and 1961 the Minx was built under licence in Japan by the Isuzu company.

From 1957 onwards, the Rootes-owned **Singer** model known as the Gazelle had a Minx-type hull, and the Minx engine was adopted two years later. In 1963 a larger car, the Super Minx, joined the range, and a new challenger in the small-car class came in the Imp, made in the Rootes Group Scottish factory at Linwood, near Glasgow. (The Ryton plant was due for expansion, but the plans were frowned upon by the Government, so a new factory was built at Linwood instead, purely to ease the unemployment situation in that area.)

The little 875-c.c. Imp would prove itself as a fine competition car during the following seasons. Both Sunbeam and Singer versions followed, as well as an estate-car version called the Husky. The engine would also go on to be used by several specialist manufacturers. If only there had not been so many teething troubles in the early examples, the Imp could well have achieved the sales that were expected of it. In the event, the Imp cost Rootes a great deal, not only in terms of development costs, but also in reputation.

Sunbeam

The Sunbeam marque originated from John Marston's tin-plate and japan-ware firm. They started making bicycles in 1887, and had built their first car within just twelve years. Enough of the company's history can be picked up from the family tree (see p.88) and, since it was not originally a Coventry company, we shall not dwell on the subject. A superb sporting history, and the fact that several Sunbeam World Land Speed Record cars took the title during the 1920s, gained the company an excellent reputation, though this wasn't enough to stop it becoming part of the Rootes Group in the mid-thirties. (Perhaps surprisingly, SS Cars had also put in a bid for the business.)

Sunbeam and Talbot were bought by the Rootes Group after the S–T–D combine went bust in 1935. The West London-built Talbot 75 spelt the end of Talbot as a specialist marque, and the final nail in the coffin came when Rootes

A very pretty 1935 Hillman Aero Minx

PEP, POWER, PERFORMANCE
says Jack Brabham

SUNBEAM ALPINE

"I can think of nothing better in driving than putting the Alpine through its paces", says Jack Brabham, World Champion Racing Driver 1959-60. "Here's everything you look for in a sports car – pep, power, performance – sensitive handling – flashing acceleration from the 1.6 litre engine – phenomenal stopping power from the front disc brakes. If, like me, you want to enjoy **going** as well as **arriving**, the Sunbeam Alpine is your car. See your Rootes Dealer for a free trial run and find out what great fun driving can be."

OPTIONAL EXTRAS : OVERDRIVE, HARD-TOP, WIRE WHEELS, WHITEWALL TYRES, FIVE COLOUR SCHEMES.   **£695 plus Purchase Tax**

By Appointment to Her Majesty The Queen
Motor Vehicle Manufacturers
Rootes Motors Limited

ROOTES MOTORS LTD SUNBEAM-TALBOT LTD., COVENTRY. LONDON SHOWROOMS AND EXPORT DIVISION
ROOTES LTD., DEVONSHIRE HOUSE, PICCADILLY, LONDON, W.1.

1925 Sunbeam Tiger powered by a 4-litre supercharged V12 engine

An outstanding pair of Sunbeams

amalgamated Sunbeam and Talbot in 1938 to form Sunbeam-Talbot Ltd.

Sunbeam-Talbot Ltd came to Coventry just after the Second World War, with production taking place at the Ryton works. Before and during the war, the first Rootes-built Sunbeam-Talbots were basically luxury fast touring cars, based on the current Hillman and Humber models, distinguished by Talbot radiators, wheel discs and metallic coachwork colours.

The first Coventry Sunbeam-Talbot was the 'Ten', but there was also a 2-litre 56-b.h.p. car that had been announced in 1940. Because of the war, its production had obviously had to be postponed. These models were replaced in 1948 by more modern vehicles of a similar type. The smaller '80' model had been discontinued by 1950, but the '90', with its wrap-round windscreens, steering-column gear-change and hypoid back axle, continued to be the company's staple product for several years. By the time production of the 90 finally came to an end, it had gained independent front suspension, as well as a more powerful 70-b.h.p. engine.

Post-war cars bound for France had been badged simply as Sunbeams, to avoid confusion with the Talbot-Lagos, but when the Alpine roadster was announced in 1953, it too was marketed as a Sunbeam, regardless of which country it was destined for. For the 1955 trading season, the saloons were renamed Sunbeam Mark IIIs, though even this would not spell the end of the Talbot.

The Sunbeam Alpine was continually developed until 1968, by which time it was designated the Alpine V. Also produced in the later years was the Sunbeam Tiger. This was powered by a large Ford V8, which caused considerable embarrassment to Chrysler when they took over the Rootes Group shortly afterwards!

Singer

The Singer Co. was founded by George Singer in 1874. Like so many of the earlier Coventry marques, Singer first built bicycles, tricycles and motorcycles, before eventually deciding to join the growing ranks of motor-car producers. The first vehicles came in 1905, and were built under licence to a Lea-Francis design. Powered by underfloor engines of either 8 or 12 h.p., these early models were soon replaced by more conventional two-, three- and four-cylinder cars using White & Poppe or Aster proprietary units.

The company actually went into receivership in 1908, but in the following year it was re-formed as Singer & Co. (1909) Ltd. Unfortunately, Singer, who was once Lord Mayor of Coventry, died in the same year.

George Singer, founder of the Singer company

Singer Ten (c. 1914)

Probably the most significant model to leave the Canterbury Street factory in those early days was the 1.1-litre 'Ten', of 1912 vintage. It was very light and economical, and was almost certainly the best British buy on the market at that time. It went on to become one of Britain's finest and most successful pre-war light cars.

The Singer Ten gained a certain amount of success in competition. A nice story attached to it tells how Lionel Martin named his cars after the Aston Clinton hill climb which he had entered in his slightly tuned Singer. Aston Martin cars would later become famous on a world-wide scale. By now, the date had been dropped from the company title, making it once again simply Singer & Co. Ltd.

After the First World War, the production of Singer motorcycles ceased. It was around this time that another company, Coventry Premier, also stopped building their two-wheeled machines, at least in this country.

Originally known as Hillman & Herbert, and later as Hillman, Herbert & Cooper Ltd (*see* p.79) the Read Street-

based company of **Coventry Premier** moved into motorcycle manufacture around 1908, while continuing with their bicycle production. At this time, the firm was known simply as **Premier**, as were its machines. Works were spread far and wide, in Germany, Austria and even Japan. The former two branches went on to make cars themselves; the German factory built the Kaiser and Premier cars, and the Austrian works built the Omega.

Coventry's first entry into the cyclecar market came in 1912 with a light four-wheeled vehicle, powered by a transverse air-cooled V-twin of 7/9-h.p. rating. This drove a two-speed gearbox via a chain, and final drive was also transmitted to the wheels by chain.

For the 1914 season, a new four-cylinder light car was introduced, featuring a three-speed gearbox and shaft drive. In November 1914 the company adopted the name of Coventry Premier.

In 1913 the factory had engaged the services of an ex-Clément-Talbot man, G.W.A. Brown, to produce a small

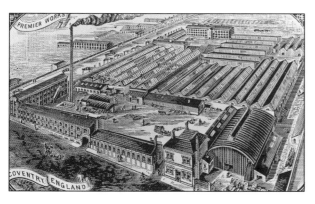

Drawing of the original Premier works, Coventry, dating from around 1895

Coventry Premier (c. 1922)

car. Six years later, the vehicle at last made its debut. The Coventry Premier was basically a three-wheeled cyclecar, which seemed unusual at the time, as most other manufacturers were using four wheels. However, it was powered by a water-cooled V-twin unit, with final drive being transmitted by chain. Shortly after production started, the chain drive was discontinued, and a three-speed (and reverse), sliding-pinion gearbox with drive-shaft was used.

1913 10.5-h.p. Calcott

Singer managed to purchase the Premier business in 1920, and the car's features began to take on more of a light-car look, for it reappeared sporting a wheel at each corner. By the following year, the vehicle had gained the Singer four-cylinder o.h.v. engine, and was marketed as a cheaper version of the Singer Ten. It sold quite well for a little while, but sales soon dried up, and when Singer found that their range was getting a little too complex, the Coventry Premier vanished.

Another Coventry business that Singer managed to buy was that of the **Calcott** brothers. This happened in 1926. The company founded by the Calcott brothers was typical of the makes that sprung to life at the start of the so-called 'motoring-for-the-masses boom' but faded away owing to stiff competition from the more efficient producers.

Calcott was also another of those companies that had progressed from bicycle and motorcycle manufacture through to car-building. It was founded in 1886, when it was known as Calcott Bros & West (the West name was dropped when Enoch West left to build up his own business), and became a limited company ten years later. Other early work included making components for such companies as Siddeley-Deasy, and a new factory was soon needed.

The first Calcott cars were built in Far Gosford Street in 1913. They provided roomy, reliable and reasonably priced transport, with all models using side-valve engines. The Calcott radiator was very similar in design to those of the Standard cars, but there the similarity ends – the total production figure for the company was only about 2500 cars! Most of that total was made up by the well-known 'Ten'. The Ten, a direct development of an earlier light car, was introduced in 1914, and it stayed in production for over a decade.

Without a doubt, Calcott, because of its relatively late entry into the field, benefitted greatly from the pioneering work of others. In addition, the car market was expanding rapidly, and the company's light car proved so successful that all vehicles had to be paid for in advance.

The 2-litre 'Twelve' and six-cylinder 2½-litre 'Sixteen' were far less popular, and very few were ever sold. Both had four forward speeds, and the Sixteen, intended for wealthy owners, was quite capable of covering a mile a minute. When William Calcott, the company's chairman, died in 1924, he left behind a business that would struggle without his leadership. The machinery was in need of replacement, too, which led to customer dissatisfaction and caused unnecessary expense. The final batch of Calcott vehicles was built in 1926, and Singer acquired the factory in the same year.

By 1927, Singer had introduced its famous four-cylinder o.h.c. engine, and fitted it to a model known as the 'Junior'. This car took Singer into the baby-car market, and into direct competition with the likes of the Austin Seven. Eventually, both four- and six-cylinder models would sport this type of valve-gear, which had already been recognized as being the most efficient. AGA of Germany negotiated with Singer to build Singer cars under licence, but nothing ever came of this.

The Singer Nine made its debut in 1932. Although

An excellent 1934 Singer Nine Le Mans

produced in only relatively small numbers, the car was an immediate success in motor sport. A works-entered Singer Nine even made an assault on the 1933 Le Mans 24 Hour Race, their first car home finishing in a very respectable thirteenth position overall – not bad for a 972 c.c. car! Following this success, most of the cars sold thereafter were 'Le Mans' sports cars.

In 1934, Singer acquired an old BSA factory in Birmingham in order to expand. The building layout was totally unsuitable for motor-car production, however, and the purchase proved to be a bad decision. This dramatic reversal of fortunes led the firm to the brink of bankruptcy. Fortunately, the company was rescued and re-formed as Singer Motors in 1937.

It was around this time that Singer tried to move into the commercial vehicle field, but again they were rewarded with very little success. Even the luxury 'Airstream', which had been inspired by the Tatra, failed to sell in any quantity, and many were later fitted with more conventional bodies, just to move them from the factory.

The marque never really made it back into its former position near the top of the manufacturers' table, and with increasing sales competition coming from such companies as Morris and Ford, along with some bad publicity gained in the Ulster TT race, when the cars suffered from steering failure, it was really only the Le Mans models that were keeping Singer afloat.

The sale of engines to HRG and Nicholas Straussler did bring in a certain amount of money just before the war, but by then, production had shifted towards the war effort. The Nine Roadster introduced in 1939 continued to be built and developed after the war, with a final version leaving the factory in 1952, by which time the Coventry works had closed.

Singer SM1500, currently on display in the Museum of British Road Transport. Its engine is of the same type as the one displayed on the right.

Neither the Second World War nor the ugly SM1500 helped matters for the ailing company, and the Rootes Group added the marque to their already massive empire in 1956. All further Singers were just badge-engineered Rootes products (William Rootes had served his apprenticeship at Singer, incidentally), and the Singer name was finally put to rest in 1970.

Chrysler acquired a majority interest in Rootes during 1964. The French authorities had allowed Chrysler to purchase Simca, and this company, along with the Japanese firm Mitsubishi, would eventually become part of the gigantic American concern.

New models to replace the old Hillman Minx and Super Minx were hurriedly designed, and the new Minx and Hunter appeared in 1967. Although the designs were

completely new, the 1496-c.c. and 1725-c.c. engines were retained. The Hunters were also assembled in Iran, under the name of Pekyan, as well as in South Africa, where Peugeot engines were used. In competition, a Hunter gained an outright victory on the 1968 London to Sydney Marathon, and this car still resides in Coventry, at the Transport Museum.

The Hillman Avenger made its debut in 1970, the same year that the Minx was dropped from the range. It was the Hunter De Luxe that replaced the Minx after an unbroken run of thirty-eight years. The Avenger could be specified with either a 1248-c.c. or 1496-c.c. four-cylinder o.h.v. engine, and, at a basic price of only £765, proved to be a highly successful motor car. It immediately outsold both the Mini and the Escort.

Avengers were later sold on the American market, badged as Plymouth Crickets. An estate version followed in 1972, along with the high-performance Avenger Tiger, built only in limited numbers. From September 1976, however, the existing Hillman Hunters and Avengers were all badged as Chryslers.

Although just a couple of years earlier the Government had had to step in to save the company (as well as British Leyland), 1978 saw the introduction of a new model, the Chrysler Sunbeam, an all-new but conventional car using a 928-c.c. development of the Hillman Imp engine. Of unitary construction, the body style was that of a three-door hatchback. Optional power units would include a 1.3 and a 1.6 litre, to be followed in 1979 by a Lotus variant. This model had a 2.2-litre twin-o.h.c. engine, with sixteen valves. It was fitted with a five-speed close-ratio gearbox, and, being

This Hillman Hunter won the 1968 London–Sydney Marathon.

One of the last Avengers – this one is badged as a Talbot. Detail changes were made to the model throughout its life, but it retained its basic design.

capable of around 120 m.p.h. proved itself admirably on the rally circuits. The Sunbeam continued to be sold until 1982, when it was replaced by the Talbot Samba.

Also produced in Coventry was the French Chrysler (Simca) model, the Alpine. With the purchase of Chrysler U.K. by the Peugeot-Citroën Group in August 1978, all models were once again renamed, this time changing to **Talbot,** a name descending from the Clément-Talbot company of the early 1900s.

Clément-Talbot was a company backed by the Earl of Shrewsbury and Talbot, and the French car-maker Adolphe Clément. It was founded in London, in October 1902, to import the Clément vehicles, but before long production was being carried out in the capital. However, the French Gladiator-built cars continued to be brought into the country by E.H. Lancaster.

The name of the selling company was changed in 1907 to the **Clément All British Motor Co.,** and the sale of their cars began in the following year. They were actually built in the Swift factory in Coventry, and bore more than a passing resemblance to the Swift models – only the slightly longer wheelbase and Talbot-like radiator (as well as the much higher prices!) set them apart.

Initially, the range consisted of a 10/12-h.p. twin, complemented by 14/18- and 18/28-h.p. four-cylinder models. In addition, two larger models, a 25/35 and a 35/45, were available. The specification for these last two vehicles was identical to that of the Gladiator models, so they were almost certainly imported straight from France. The range continued much the same until around 1911, when the two larger cars were being sold under the marque name of Gladiator.

The Talbot Alpine

Period shot of a 1903 Clement with Vesta Tilley, a music-hall performer, at the wheel

By 1913, the 'twin' had been dropped, and two four-cylinder cars made up the Clément range: a 12/14 and a 14/18, these again being similar to the Swifts on offer at the time. For 1914, though, a totally new 16/20-h.p. car was introduced. In 1919 the British-owned Société Alexandre Darracq acquired the Clément business and, shortly afterwards, Sunbeam, thus forming the Sunbeam–Talbot–Darracq group. Later, of course, the combine would become a part of the massive Rootes empire.

An Alpine derivative, the Solara, was also built in Coventry, as was the Horizon, a small family hatchback. It was left to these models, along with the Alpine and Samba, to keep the Talbot marque alive.

The French parent company invested many millions of pounds in the Coventry sites in the 1980s. Their reward was the first British-built Peugeot, introduced in January 1986.

The Peugeot 205 T16 proved to be an excellent rally car, winning the world championship in 1985 and 1986.

This model, known as the '309', has proved to be quite a success story. The larger, up-market '405' followed in October 1987, and was immediately awarded the title of 'International Car of the Year 1988'. Once these new Peugeots had made their mark on the British market, the Talbot range was deleted, but at present the French are showing a great deal of faith in, and commitment to, the city's factories. Hopefully this will continue for many years to come. Below is a family tree showing where all the companies fit into the story.

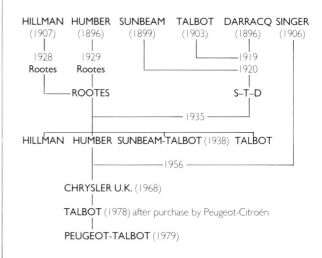

The Peugeot 405 (left) and 309 GTi.

12

THE JAGUAR GROUP

JAGUAR BEGAN LIFE AS A PRESTIGIOUS AND HIGH-PERFORMANCE MARQUE, A REPUTATION IT HAS MAINTAINED EVER SINCE. AFTER DIFFICULTIES IN THE 1970s THE COMPANY SPRANG BACK INTO PROMINENCE IN THE 1980s.

> Swallow/SS/SS Jaguar, *Holbrook Lane, 1928–1945*
> Jaguar, *Browns Lane, 1945–*

William Lyons was born in Blackpool on 4 September 1901. Despite originally wanting to go into shipbuilding, he would devote his life to the automobile trade, moving to Crossley Motors in 1918. He was always a keen motor-cyclist, owning and racing several different machines. This interest would serve him well in the future.

After buying a side-car from a Blackpool neighbour, Lyons suggested a partnership with its builder, William Warmsley. Together they set up a business known as the Swallow Sidecar Co. In a very short space of time, extra premises were needed. Eventually one very large building was obtained, and the company was renamed the Swallow Sidecar and Coach Building Co.

People moved up from the Midlands to work for this new firm, which even then seemed to be going places. The Midlanders brought with them the knowledge and experience that were necessary for the company to grow still more. Soon the firm would be building its own bodies for the popular chassis of the time.

The need to expand further meant another move. This time, though, it was a little further afield, and Swallow came to Coventry on 7 November 1928. A disused shell-filling factory on the Whitmore Park Estate was leased, and an option on two more buildings in the block was granted. The road to the new site would eventually be called Swallow Road.

Swallow were to build on several different makers' chassis, Austin, Morris, Fiat, Alvis, Wolseley and Swift among them, but by far the most important connection made in those early days was the one with Standard.

It was more than likely Standard who leaked to *The Autocar* magazine news of a new two-seater coupé that Lyons was working on. It put pressure on the company but,

Sir William Lyons, founder of Jaguar Cars Ltd

A delightful little Austin Swallow. Production began in Blackpool, and then Swallow moved down to Coventry.

The magnificent SS1

The SS100, the first car to carry the Jaguar name

Surely one of the most glamorous Jaguar creations, the XK120. The XK140 and XK150 followed, taking the type to 1960, and to a total of 30357 cars.

none the less, the car was ready for the 1931 Olympia show. The SS1 was almost certainly the star of the show, and soon afterwards, production models were rolling from the factory.

In late October 1933 William Lyons registered a subsidiary company, SS Cars Ltd. Development work would be carried out under this name. Warmsley resigned from the firm in 1935, the same year that SS Cars became a public company. The Swallow Coachbuilding Co. (1935) Ltd was formed to deal with the side-car business, and SS was officially made the dominant marque of the company.

After some thought, it was decided that the name 'SS' no longer meant anything. An advertising agency was called in, and suggested the title of **Jaguar.** This name appealed to Lyons, and so it was that the new SS Jaguar range was launched, in Sepember 1935. The range as a whole was very beautiful, but it is the SS100 that must surely be remembered as the most outstanding car of the pre-war models. The firm took over Motor Panels (Coventry) Ltd just before the war, but later sold the business to Rubery Owen. Despite this, Motor Panels have close links with the Jaguar marque to this day.

During the war, the factory received a large number of contracts and produced an amazing amount of parts that would help towards the war effort. The bonds with Standard were severed when the company managed to purchase the machine tools for producing the 2.7- and 3.5-litre engines, and Sir John Black then used Triumph to try to recapture some of the market that SS had a strong hold on. When the war finally ended, the name of Jaguar Cars Ltd had been approved. William Lyons' dream was at last realized.

Much has been written about Lyons and his men designing the post-war range of cars and engines whilst fire-watching during the Blitz, and a lot of it is quite true. The Mark V would appear, and, much more importantly, so would the legendary twin-cam XK engine. The first time the public saw it was in four-cylinder guise, when it powered the Gardner Special to take speed records on a Belgian motorway in 1948. Its next appearance was in the now familiar six-cylinder form, fitted to the show-stopping XK120 – without doubt, one of the most beautiful cars ever built.

The company already had an excellent competition history, and the XK engine would help keep the tradition

A Jaguar C-type on its way to victory in the 1951 Le Mans 24-Hour Race. This was the first of five Le Mans victories for Jaguar during the 1950s. On this occasion the drivers were Peter Whitehead and Peter Walker.

going. Although not originally designed for racing, it was undeniably powerful enough to be used for that purpose. Ron 'Soapy' Sutton had taken an XK120 to over 130 m.p.h. in Jabbeke – it was enough to prompt the factory into forming a works team, and it was here, that Jaguar's illustrious racing era began.

With the launch of the Mark VII saloon, Jaguar once again needed to expand, the demand for the marque's products being very high. Lyons couldn't obtain permission to build between the existing factory and Beake Avenue, so another major move was necessary. Negotiations were completed to lease the Daimler Number Two Shadow Factory in Browns Lane, Allesley, and by the end of 1951, much of the operation at Swallow Road had been successfully transferred to the new plant.

The fifties would be dominated by the motor-sport exploits of the company. Jaguar had no less than five Le Mans victories in the decade with the immensely successful purpose-built C- and D-type racing cars.

The Mark I compact saloon was introduced in 1955, and William Lyons became Sir William in the following year. The racing programme was suspended due to new regulations, and it was decided to concentrate on saloon cars. Late in 1959, the Mark II, a 'face-lift' of the Mark I, was introduced, and this was to be one of the best loved of all the Jaguar saloons, particularly in 3.8-litre form.

The very collectable Mark II Jaguar

Mid-way through June 1960, Jaguar purchased from the Birmingham Small Arms Co. (BSA) the Daimler name and business, along with the factory at Radford. This allowed Jaguar to expand substantially, but at a cost of £3.4 million. The plan was to move all car production to Browns Lane, while retaining commercial and military vehicle operations at Radford. Machining and engine-building would also be confined to the Radford works.

The E-type Jaguar, one of Britain's most successful sports cars, was produced between 1961 and 1975.

Lyons wanted to branch out into the commercial field, so he arranged for a Daimler truck to be designed. A prototype was built, the first Daimler truck for many years, but it was also to be the last, as Jaguar bought the Wolverhampton-based Guy Motors in 1961. Two magnificent Jaguars were launched in the same year, one was the E-type, and the other the Mark X. The E-type was to become the ultimate sports-car, whilst the Mark X set new saloon-car standards.

Towards the end of 1962, the 2½-litre V8 saloon was introduced. This employed a Mark II body-shell and the delightful small Daimler V8 engine. This was the first of several badge-engineered Jaguar-Daimlers, with the Daimler usually being marketed as the top-of-the-range model.

Coventry Climax became part of the Jaguar Group in March 1963. Climax, although perhaps more famous for their fork-lift trucks and fire pumps, in fact had an extraordinary racing history. Their engines powered many Grand Prix cars, and helped such teams as Lotus, Cooper and Brabham to nearly 100 victories in the late fifties and sixties. Walter Hassan, who had previously worked for Jaguar, found himself back with them again, and another fine engineer, Harry Mundy, also came from Climax. Like Jaguar, the firm would regain its independence in the early eighties, freed from Leyland's grip.

Many people had noted that the company were making

The XJ6, often described as 'the best car in the world'. This is a Series One model, first produced in 1968.

too many different saloon models. This was actually a deliberate Jaguar policy, but things would change dramatically with the introduction of the ultimate vehicle, the XJ. Sir William believed everything was going to work out when Jaguar merged with the British Motor Corporation.

British Leyland became operational around a month before the launch of the new Daimler DS420 limousine. This beautiful car is still in production today, and has changed very

Coventry's mayoral carriage, a Daimler DS420

version the Double-Six. The XJ12 was powered by a supremely smooth V12 engine of 5.3 litres, giving the car a top speed of around 150 m.p.h. Like the XK power unit, which continues to be built for military applications, the V12 is still in production today, although both have been greatly modified over the years.

Geoffrey Robinson was called in to run the company in time for the Series II XJ launch in 1973. Lofty would retire less than five months later, but Robinson didn't last much longer with Jaguar. Leyland very nearly destroyed Jaguar and Daimler, with only a small bunch of enthusiasts within the company managing to keep the marque alive.

In 1975 the much-loved E-type Jaguar was replaced by the V12-powered XJ-S. Although it was not the immediate success that other models from the famous stable had been, in its later forms this model is regarded as one of the very best cars in the world. The survival of the XJ-S is due largely to the marketing of the HE (High Efficiency) V12 engine introduced in mid-1981, which produced more power, but with better fuel economy.

By 1978, the Leyland heirarchy had decided to revive marque names, and eventually Jaguar was combined with the other 'specialists', Triumph and Rover. This situation lasted for only a couple of years, and morale hit an all-time low at Browns Lane. John Egan joined Jaguar in 1980, and manged to do exactly what he had set out to do – to turn the company back into something to be proud of, as well as making it profitable.

Leyland had made an effort to return to the race-track but it was largely unsuccessful. In America, though, a car loosely based on the ill-fated XJ13 prototype was doing rather well.

little since it was first seen in June 1968. Royalty have started to support the marque again through this model, which is still hand-built by skilled Jaguar craftsmen.

Sir William's finest hour must have been the launch of the XJ6 in September 1968. Within two years, the whole saloon range was XJ-based, and included an attractive Daimler version, the Sovereign, introduced nearly a year after the Jaguars.

Owing to the corporate policies of British Leyland, Jaguar Cars Ltd ceased to be a separate company in 1972. Thankfully, though, it did at least retain its identity. Lofty England, who had joined the company in 1946, was to succeed Sir William as chairman, and after the introduction of the legendary XJ12, it was his decision to name the Daimler

The Jaguar XJ-S 3.6-litre coupé

Sir John Egan, Chairman and Chief Executive of Jaguar

Back at home, a team of Tom Walkinshaw-prepared XJ-S models was campaigned, and eventually a new works racing programme was developed.

The AJ6 3.6-litre engine was first seen in late 1983, and just a few months later, Jaguar would once again go into private ownership. The company finally went on the stock-market in August 1984. Massive profits had just been reported, and the XJ-Ss had recently won a major event. It was also to be a record year for production.

The founder of the company, Sir William Lyons, passed away in 1985. He died peacefully at his Warwickshire home at the age of 83. Happier news came in the following year, when the XJR-6 scored its first victory – the marque's first win in a world championship sports car race since the famous 1957 Le Mans race. Jaguar would return there, too. A month after Le Mans, John Egan was knighted, and in October, the British launch of the project code-named XJ40 dominated the headlines.

Jaguar became the 1987 World Sports Car Champions, proving that the legend was still very much alive. This feat was repeated the following year, and the illustrious Le Mans title was at last Jaguar's, after a gap of over thirty years.

A new development site at Whitley, once the property of Peugeot-Talbot, shows Jaguar's commitment to the future, and a newly formed subsidiary called Jaguar Sport should ensure that many more exciting vehicles will come from what is now one of the leading companies in the industry. The marque has returned to its original purpose, to provide high performance and exceptional quality for a very reasonable amount of money. The latest super-car from Coventry – the XJ220 – will keep the German manufacturers in second place for quite some time. A limited run of XJ220s will be built by Abbey Panels in the very near future. It should be remembered that Abbey Panels built the chassis for the famous Ford racing car, the GT40, of the mid- and late 1960s.

Towards the end of 1989 came the news of a potential Jaguar takeover bid by General Motors of America. Ford were more than interested in the marque as well, and both Mercedes-Benz and BMW were waiting on the side-lines to see what would happen.

Eventually, Ford managed to obtain a majority holding in the company, though it is thought that Jaguar will remain very much an independent business, but with a lot more capital at their disposal to develop new models.

The XJ40 in its ultimate form: the Daimler 3.6. In 1989 the engine was up-rated to 4 litres, giving it even smoother high performance.

APPENDIX I

CAR MANUFACTURERS

The following is a complete list of Coventry's car manufacturers, past and present. The dates in brackets indicate the approximate year in which they first built cars under the given marque name. The history of all these companies is well documented within the main chapters.

Academy (1906)
Acme (1919)
Aircraft (1919)
Albatros (1923)
Allard (1898)
Alpha (1914)
Alvis (1920)
Arden (1912)
Ariel (1900)
Armstrong-Siddeley (1919)
Arno (1908)
Aurora (1903)
Auto-Forge Automobiles (1987)
Autovia (1936)
Awson (1926)
Barnett (1921)
Bayliss, Thomas (1920)
Beeston (1899)
Billings (1900)
Bramco (1921)
British Motor Co. (1896)
British Motor Traction (1906)
Broadway (1913)
Brooks (1901)
Buckingham (1913)
Calcott (1913)
Carbodies (1946)
Carlton (1901)
Centaur (1900)
Challenge (1912)
Chrysler U.K. (1968)
Clarendon (1902)
Clément (1908)
Climax (1905)
Cluley (1922)
Cooper (1922)
Coronet (1903)
Coventry Premier (1913)
Coventry Victor (1926)
Crouch (1912)
Daimler (1896)
Dalton & Wade (1906)
Dawson (1919)
Deasy (1906)
Doherty (1906)
Duryea (1902)

Eagle (1912)
Emms (1922)
Endurance (1899)
Ferguson (1950)
Forge (1903)
Forman (1901)
Garrard & Blumfield (1894)
Glover (1912)
Great Horseless Carriage Co. (1896)
Hamilton (1903)
Hillman (1910)
Hillman-Coatalen (1907)
Hobart Bird (1904)
Hotchkiss (1920)
Hubbard (1906)
Humber (1896)
Iden (1904)
Jaguar (1945)
Lady (1899)
Lanchester (1931)
Lea-Francis (1904)
Lee-Stroyer (1903)
Lotis (1908)
Marseal (1919)
Maudslay (1901)
John McGuire Racing (1977)
Motor Manufacturing Co. (1898)
Motor Radiator (1912)
New Beeston (1898)
Omega (1925)
Payne & Bates (1900)
Pennington (1896)
Peugeot-Talbot (1979)
Progress (1899)
Raglan (1899)
Ranger (1913)
Record (1905)
Remington (1919)
Rex (1902)
Ridley (1901)
Riley (1898)
Andy Rouse Engineering (1983)
Rover (1904)
Rudge (1912)
Ryley (1901)

Siddeley (1902)
Siddeley-Deasy (1911)
Singer (1900)
Standard (1903)
Stoneleigh (1912)
Sunbeam-Talbot (1946)
Swallow/SS/SS Jaguar (1928)
Swift (1899)
Talbot (1978)
Taylor-Swetnam (1913)

Titan (1911)
Triumph (1923)
Velox (1902)
Viking (1914)
Warwick (1926)
West-Aster (1904)
Whitley (1900)
Wigan Barlow (1922)
Williamson (1913)

Donald **Healey** had offices in Canterbury Street, Coventry during the late sixties and early seventies. It was around this time that Healey became involved with the Jensen brothers in West Bromwich.

Austin-Rover still occupy the old Standard factory sites between Canley and Tile Hill, where the group houses its Headquarters, Product and Engineering section, Fleet Sales, and Sales and Marketing divisions, although the organization is now known as the Rover Group.

In February 1984, the front page of the *Coventry Evening Telegraph* carried the news that **Honda** wanted to come to England, Coventry being one of the first sites the Japanese company would consider for their new factory. Unfortunately, the initial negotiations led no further.

Imperial Motor Cars of Eastbourne planned to move their operations to Coventry in mid-1988 and take over part of an old factory in Mason Road, Foleshill, thus creating 300 new jobs. However, talks between Shire Textiles, the owners of the building, and the Imperial board failed only days after the venture had been announced. It was hoped that the Jackel sports car could have been built alongside the firm's 'olde-worlde' delivery vans and small coaches.

In 1989 the Japanese company **Toyota** was looking to build a new plant in England. A site near Baginton Airport was considered quite seriously, but unfortunately, space there was restricted, and Toyota bought cheaper land in the North.

Although the deal with Toyota was lost, **Proton** Cars (U.K.) Ltd did come to Coventry. The Proton was Malaysia's first car, and was introduced into Great Britain at the 1988 Motor Show. The company's offices were set up in Mile Lane, just opposite Kalmar-Climax, to handle the importation of the Proton Saga as the United Kingdom's sole concessionaires. However, due to the success of the company, larger premises became necessary, and Proton were forced to move to nearby Birmingham in late 1989.

The Proton range of four-door saloons and five-door aeroback models made their U.K. debut at the 1988 Motor Show, where they won two medals in the international coachwork competition.

APPENDIX II

ENGINE BUILDERS

The following is a list of all Coventry's engine-building firms, past and present.

Aero and Marine Engine Co., Stoney Stanton Road
Aircraft, Shackleton Road
Arden, Balsall Common
Barnett, High Street
British Motor Co. Ltd, Drapers Field
Carlton, Lockhurst Lane
Climax Engines Ltd, Bulls Head Lane
Condor Motor Co., Broad Street
Coventry Climax Engines Ltd, East Street
Coventry Diesel Engines Ltd, Friars Road
Coventry Simplex Engine Co., Paynes Lane
Coventry Victor Motor Co. Ltd, Cox Street
Cromwell Engineering Co., Chauntry Place
Cunard, Leicester Street
Daimler Motor Co. Ltd, Drapers Field
Daisy, Far Gosford Street
Dutson-Ward, Gosford Street
Endurance, Gosford Street
Forman Motor Co., High Street
Gulson Engineering Co. Ltd, Gulson Road Works
Hillman Motor Co. Ltd, Humber Road
Hotchkiss, Courthouse Green
J. E. Motors, Siskin Drive
Johnson, Hurley & Martin, Alpha Motor Works, Gosford Street
Lea-Francis Cars Ltd, Much Park Street
Lee, Stroyer & Co., East Street
Morris Motors (1926) Ltd, Gosford Street
Morris Motors Ltd, Courthouse Green
Motor Accessories Co., Broad Street
NCK Racing, Bedworth Road
Payne & Co., Castle Street
Record, Stoney Stanton Road
Remington, Foleshill Road
Ryley Engine Co. Ltd, Aldbourne Road
Simplex Engine Co., East Street
Transport Vehicles (Daimler) Ltd, Radford Works
Victor Oil Engines Co., Harefield Road
White & Poppe, Lockhurst Lane

Note: It must be remembered that companies such as Standard and Jaguar also supplied engines to other clients, but in most cases, any major dealings are described in the relevant chapters of this book.

White & Poppe

The story of some of the above engine-builders – for example, Coventry Climax, Hotchkiss and Morris – is told in the main chapters of this book. The widely respected firm of White & Poppe, however, is mentioned only in passing. The company was created at the end of the nineteenth century by Alfred White, a watchmaker, and Peter Poppe.

Swift had placed a large order for White & Poppe engines in 1905, and this proved to be a turning-point for the company, as many other car-builders followed suit, placing their orders shortly afterwards. During the First World War, White & Poppe were engaged in making carburettors and light-car engines. However, this work ceased almost at once when they received a contract to manufacture and supply 10000 fuse-bodies and eighteen-pounder sockets each week. White & Poppe were bought by Dennis Brothers of Guildford at the end of 1919. The reason for the sale seems to have been a disagreement between the partners concerning a proposal to go into car production.

Grahame Bryant stands proudly beside his race-winning Morgan. The Rover V8 engine was modified, built and tuned by J.E. Motors, a company founded by John Eales in 1976.

Between 1986 and 1989 J.E. Motors supplied their highly tuned Rover V8 engines to the works Paris–Dakar Rally Land Rovers and Range Rovers. Results were consistently good.

APPENDIX III

THE COACH-BUILDING TRADE

As one would expect with such a thriving industry, many companies were set up to complement Coventry's car manufacturers: engine-builders, accessory manufacturers and of course coachwork specialists and body-builders. After the Second World War, the trade died out, mainly due to the mass-production methods employed by the factories at the time. Below is a complete listing of all the city's coach-builders, past and present.

Companies founded before the Second World War:

Acme Motor Co., Osborn Road
Atkinson, S.F., Highland Road
Awson Motor Carriage Co., Awson Street
Bradnick, R.H., Far Gosford Street
British Pressed Panel Co., Edward Road
Bryant, E., North Street
Burlington Carriage Co., Parkside
Butlin, J.H., All Saints Lane
Cammell, C. & Co., Ordnance Road
Carbodies, Hill Street
Carbodies, Holyhead Road
Charlesworth Bodies, Much Park Street
City Carriage Works, Lamb Street
Cliff Bros, Brighton Street
Coventry Hood & Sidescreen Co., Cheylesmore
Coventry Motor & Sundries, Spon End
Coventry Motor Bodies, Cow Lane
Coventry Supply Garage, Holyhead Road
Cross & Edwards Ltd., Clay Lane
Cross & Ellis, Clay Lane
Curle Bros, Stoney Stanton Road
Death, H., Fairfield Terrace
Dunn & Ensor, Cross Cheaping
Earlsdon Motor Body & Carriage Works, Moor Street
Eaves & Barratt, The Barracks
Eaves, H. & Son, Earlsdon Street
Ediss & Son, Earlsdon Street
Edwards, F., Foleshill Road
Fisher & Ludlow, Station Road
Fleet Works Carriage Co., Fleet Street
Foleshill Motor and Carriage Works, Stoney Stanton Road
Garrett, F., Lamb Street
General Automobile Panels, Moor Street
Guild & Grunau, Awson Street
Hancock & Warman, Walsgrave Road
Harvey, J., Far Gosford Street
Hawkins & Peake, Bishop Street
Hewer Car Bodies, Aldbourne Road
Hobley, Thos, Chester Street
Holbrook Bodies Ltd, Holbrook Lane
Hollick, H., Barras Lane
Hollick & Pratt, Mile Lane and Smithford Street
Hough, E.C., Clay Lane

Hoyal Body Corporation Ltd, Queens Road
Mann, H., Lamb Street
Mason, Albert Henry, Sir Thomas White's Road
Midland Light Bodies, Stoke Row
Midland Light Body, Byron Street
Midland Motor Body, Aldbourne Road
Morris Motors (1926) Ltd, Quinton Road
Motor Bodies (Coventry), Holbrook Lane
Musson & Grindlay, Spon End
New Inn Bridge Carriage Works, Foleshill Road
Parkside Motor Body Works, Parkside
Parsons & Sons, Warwick Street
Pass, Thos, Little Park Street and West Orchard
Poole, H.J., Cross Cheaping
Sadler Bros, Spon Street
Sadler, T., Cox Street
Smedley & Gray Ltd, Walsgrave Road
Standard, Bishopsgate Green and Cash's Lane
Swift, Little Park Street and West Orchard
Swift of Coventry, Cheylesmore
Tarver Bros, Moor Street
Timms, W.E., The Butts
Viking Motor Co., Warwick Road
Walsgrave Motor Body Co., Walsgrave Road
Ward, W.E. & Co., Earlsdon Avenue South

Companies founded after the Second World War:

Abbey Panels Ltd, Bayton Road
Adams & Walters, Stoney Stanton Road
Barker & Co., Radford Works
Central Garage, Longford Road
Commercial Motor Body Co., Brighton Street
Coventry Garage, Holyhead Road
Laroc (Coventry) Ltd, Radford Road
Motor Panels (Coventry) Ltd, Holbrook Lane
Park Sheet Metal, Bayton Road
Scott Lewis & Co., Broad Street
Sovereign Motors, Sovereign Road
Stadium Body Repairs, Lythalls Lane
Sullivan, D., Foleshill Road
Taylor, S.G., Brighton Street

During the early part of the 1960s, an ambitious scheme was put forward by a local motor-body engineer. The idea was similar to Hitler's plans for the Volkswagen – to replace all other cars with one model. The vehicle would have been

Drawing of the proposed 'Hermes People's Car'

known as the **Hermes,** with power coming from a small o.h.c. 600-c.c. engine, but although the plan was sent to several members of Parliament, nothing ever came of it.

Thrust II, the current Land Speed Record holder, now resides in Coventry's Transport Museum. This isn't the city's only link with the Land Speed Record, for Donald Campbell's legendary Bluebird was bodied at Motor Panels, who are still trading from their factory in Holbrook Lane.

Bluebird at the Motor Panels works

The coachwork of this prototype Jaguar XJ220 is mostly by Park Sheet Metal. The work for the production models will be by Abbey Panels Ltd.

Charlesworth Bodies
LIMITED.

MUCH PARK STREET,

COVENTRY.

TELEPHONE 538

HIGH-CLASS COACH-BUILT
BODIES DESIGNED TO
SUIT ANY CHASSIS.

LANDAULETTES.
LIMOUSINES.
CHAR-A-BANCS.
DELIVERY VANS.
FOUR-SEATERS.
TWO-SEATERS.
CABS.
HOODS & SCREENS.

APPENDIX IV

CYCLE MANUFACTURERS

The dates in brackets indicate the year in which these Coventry cycle-builders first sold their machines under the name given. A question mark (?) appears where no date could be verified.

Alcester Cycle Co. Ltd (1904)
Allard & Co. (1891)
All Right Cycle Co. (1894)
Arnold, C.H. (1907)
Arrow Cycle Co. (1894)
Associated Cycle Manufacturers of Coventry Ltd (1953)
Atkins, J. (1907)
Atlas Engineering Co. (1919)
Attenborough & Underwood (1984)
Avon Cycle Co. (1898)
Balmoral Cycle Co. (1909)
Barnett, A. & Co. (1919)
Bayliss, Thomas & Co. (1879)
Bayliss, Timms & Co. (1879)
Beacon Cycle Co. (1912)
Bennett, Cotton & Co. (1894)
Birchall, W. (1907)

Bird & Co. (1919)
Bonnick & Co. Ltd (1890)
Boro Mills Co. Ltd (1894)
Boyd, C. (1898)
Brenda Cycle & Motor Co. (1921)
Britannia Cycle & Motor Co. (1929)
British Challenge Cycle Co. (1919)
Briton Cycle Co. (1898)
Bromwich Cycles Ltd (1980)
Burdess, Adam (1882)
Burdess & Townsend (1886)
Caesar Cycle Co. (1903)
Calcott Bros Ltd (1912)
Calcott Bros & West (1890)
Caroche Tricycle Co. (1880)
Centaur Bicycle & Tricycle Manufacturing Co (1879)
Centaur Cycle Co. (1911)
Central Cycle Co. (1894)

Central Manufacturing Co. (1903)
Centric Cycle Co. (1898)
Challenge Cycle Co. (1903)
Challenge Cycle & Motor Co. (1911)
Chinn, B.S. (1903)
Clarendon Motor Car & Cycle Co. (?)
Clarke, Cluley & Co. (1894)
Clarke, C.W. (1903)
Clarke, W. (1898)
Colonial Cycle Co. (1909)
Congreve, J.T.A. (1903)
Conqueror Cycle Co. (1890)
Coronet Cycle Co. (1896)
Courts, J., Lloyd & Co. (1894)
Coventry Bicycle Ltd (1921)
Coventry Cees Ltd (1939)
Coventry Chaser Cycle Co. (1898)
Coventry Co-operative Cycle Manufacturers Ltd (1898)
Coventry Cross Cycles Ltd (1896)
Coventry Cycle Co. (1883)
Coventy Cycle Factoring Co. (1921)
Coventry Eagle Cycle Co. (1911)
Coventry Ensign Cycle & Motor Co. (1919)

Coventry Hawk Cycle Co. (1931)
Coventry Herald Cycle Co. (1888)
Coventry Industries Ltd (1939)
Coventry & Midlands Cycle Co. (1890)
Coventry Machinists Co. Ltd (1869)
Coventry Majestic Cycle Co. (1923)
Coventry Mascot Cycle Co. (1922)
Coventry Progress Cycle & Rotor Co. (1921)
Coventry Trio Cycle Co. (1909)
Coventry Wheel Co. Ltd (1898)
Craven Cycle Co. Ltd (1898)
Dedicoat, John Richard (1879)
Dingley Bros (1912)
Dodwell, J. (1903)
Dolphin Cycle Co. Ltd (1896)
Dover Ltd (1937)
Dragoon Cycle Co. (1911)
Drakeford & Randle (1894)
Drakeford, Randle & Cooke (1894)
Dutson & Ward (1903)
Eales & Co. (1896)

Bayliss, Thomas 'Ordinary' cycle, c. 1880

Fitting shop at the Coventry Cross works, c. 1896

Easip Cycle Co. (1912)
Elk (Farmer & Co) (1903)
Elliot, Joseph (1912)
Elston Cycle Co. (1919)
English & Continental Cycle
    Co. (1894)
Ensign Cycle Co. (1909)
F & P Products (1953)
Flavell & Co. (1890)
Flying Monarch Cycle Co.
    (1898)
Francis & Barnett Ltd
    (1921)
Francis, W. (1898)
Fulwell & Co. Ltd (1898)
Fulwell Cycle Co. (1894)
Gallois Brown & Co. (1898)
Gibbs, R. (1903)
Gill, A.C. (1894)
Gloria Cycle Co. (1898)
Gortan, S. & B. Ltd (1890)
Griffiths, John Alfred (1884)
Grovenor, R. (1903)
Halford Cycle Co. Ltd
    (1911)
Hammerton, H.E. (1898)
Harris Cycle Co. Ltd (1903)
Hawley Cycle
    Manufacturing Co. (1898)
Hawley Junior & Co. (1896)
Hawthorne, G. (1896)
Haynes & Jefferis & Co.
    (1879)
Hazelwood's Ltd (1903)
Herbert & Hubbard (1890)
Hewitt, Loasby & Co.
    (1884)
Highway Cycle Co. (1898)
Hillman & Herberts (1879)
Hillman, Herbert & Cooper
    (1880)
Hobart, Bird & Co. Ltd
    (1898)
Holbrook Cycle Co. (1921)
Holland, J.A. & Co. (1898)
Hosier, William & Co.
    (1879)
Hotchkiss, Mayo & Meek
    (1894)
Hubbard & Sons (1912)
Humber & Co. (1890)
Iris Cycling Co. Ltd (1907)
Irving, J.S. (1903)
Ivanhoe Cycle Co. (1894)
Jacks of Earlsdon (1953)
Jackson Cycle Co. (1903)
Jelley, T.G. (1894)
Johnson, Wood & Co. (?)
Jones, E. (1894)

Jones, Venn & Co. Ltd (?)
Joyce Cycles Ltd (1926)
Keen Cycle Co. Ltd (1898)
Lake & Elliott Ltd (1933)
Lancer Cycle & Motor Co.
    (1901)
Lawson, H.J. Queen Bicycle
    Co. (1880)
Laxton & Simmons (?)
Lea-Francis Ltd (1896)
Lester, H. (1894)
Lightweight Cycles Ltd
    (1934)
Lloyd, Read & Co. (1894)
Lyceum Cycle Co. (1904)
Lynes, A.E. & Co. Ltd
    (1921)
Macklin & Sons (1898)
Male & Middleton Ltd
    (1931)
Markham & Co. (1890)
Marriot & Cooper (1894)
Martston, W.H. & Co.
    (1894)
Martlet Cycle Co. (?)
Mascot Cycle Co. (1921)
Maxim Cycle Co. (1896)
Maximum Cycle Co. Ltd
    (1926)
Mentor Cycle Co. (1903)
Meri Cycle Manufacturing
    Co. (1912)
Merlin Cycle Co. (1907)
Micrometer Cycle Co.
    (1898)
Middlemore (Coventry) Ltd
    (1953)
Midland Cycle Co. (1929)
Midland Factoring Co.
    (1953)

One of several tricycles Premier produced in the late nineteenth century

A small selection of the bicycles Vivi import from Italy

Mills & Fulford (1903)
Mizen, W.T. (1939)
Mohawk Cycle Co. (1912)
Mona Cycle Co. (1896)
Monopole Cycle & Carriage
 (1904)
Moore & Owen (1903)
National Cycle Co. Ltd
 (1889)
Nelson & Florendine (1898)
Nelson, Wright & Co.
 (1879)
New Beeston Cycle Co.
 Ltd (1896)
New Coventry Bicycle Co.
 (1903)
New Coventry Cycle Co.
 (1898)
New England Cycle Co.
 (1921)
New Premier Cycle Co.
 Ltd (1898)
New Townend Bros (1903)
Norton Cycle & Motor Co.
 (1905)
O'Brien, Edward Ltd (1970)
O'Brien Ltd (1933)
Old Robin Hood Cycle
 Works (1919)
Pearson, Hollis & Co.
 (1898)
Phoenix Bicycle & Tricycle
 (1880)
Player Bros & Co. (1896)
Pollard, W. & Co. (1923)
Premier Cycle Co. (1890)
Prentice, T.L. (1912)
Progress Cycle Co. Ltd
 (1903)
Propellor Cycle Co. (1885)
Puma Cycle Ltd (1983)
Quadrant Cycle Co. (?)
Quinton Cycle Co. (1891)
Raglan Cycle and Anti-
 Friction Ball Co. Ltd
 (1898)
Reeley Cycle Co. (1898)
Reform Cycle Co. (1894)
Reliable Cycle Co. (1921)
Remington Cycle Co.
 (1909)
Riley Cycle Co. (1896)
Roman Cycle Co. (1898)
Roulette Co. (1890)
Rover Cycle Co. (1896)
Rowing Tricycle Co. (later
 Sculler Co.) (1888)
Royal Prince Cycle Co.
 (1894)

Rudge & Co. Ltd (1886)
Rudge, Whitworth Ltd
 (1896)
Ryley, Ward & Bradford
 (1898)
Saxon Cycle Co. (1894)
Settle & Co. (1880)
Shaffir, J.H. & Co. (1896)
Shuresta Ltd (1958)
Sidney Cycle Co. (1898)
Simmons, William (1880)
Singer & Co. (1879)
Smallwood, T. & Co. (?)
Smith & Molesworth (1890)
Smith & Molesworth Ltd
 (1919)
Sparkbrook Manufacturing
 Co. Ltd (1883)
Speed Manufacturing Co.
 Ltd (1898)
Speedwell Cycle Co. (J.K.
 Rowland) (1926)
Stafford Cycle Co. Ltd
 (1898)
Stafford & Caves (?)
Standard Cycle Co. (1923)
Standard Cycle Co. (H.J.
 Leake) (1896)
Stanley Cycle Works (1898)
Starley Bros (1879)
Starley & Sutton (1879)
Stokes, George & Co.
 (1953)
Sutton & William (1879)
Swanswell Cycle Co. (1909)
Swift Cycle Co. Ltd
 (1903)
Swift, E.J. (1903)
Tangent & Coventry
 Tricycle Manufacturing
 Co. (1879)
Tansley, G. & Co. (1896)
Taylor, Cooper & Bednall
 (1889)
Thomas, Frederick J. (1879)
Timms & Co. (1880)
Townend Bros (1891)
Townend, Frank & Co.
 (1903)
Townend, G. Boys' & Girls'
 Tricycle Manufacturers
 (1880)
Triumph Cycle Co. Ltd
 (1894)
Tri-Velox Ltd (1939)
Turner, W.B. & Sons (1896)
Vernon Cycle Co. (1930)
Vernon Cycle & Motor Co.
 (1912)

Viaduct Works Cycle Co.
 (1904)
Victor Cycle Co. (1890)
Viking Cycle Co. Ltd (1894)
Vivi Engineers Ltd (1893)
Walter Hewitt Cycle Co.
 (1912)
Ward & Co. (1921)
Ward, S. (1905)
Ward, T.A. Junior (1905)
Warman & Hazelwood
 (1890)
Warman, Laxon & Co.
 (1879)
Watchman Cycle Co.
 (1894)

Wee McGregor Coventry
 Bicycles Ltd (1922)
West, E.J. (1904)
Westwood Manufacturing
 Co. (1896)
Whirlwind Cycle Co.
 (1911)
Whitehouse & Co. – Cycle
 and Motorcycle
 Manufacturers (1919)
Wilkins & Co. (1905)
Woodcock Cycle Co.
 (1896)
Wright, D. & Son (1894)
Younge Bros (1896)
Zephyr Tricycle Co.
 (1881)

Starley 'Rover' bicycle c. 1888

R.L. Jefferson with the Swift cycle he rode 2500 miles to Istanbul (then Constantinople) and back in the last century

APPENDIX V

MOTORCYCLE MANUFACTURER

The following is a list of all Coventry's motorcycle manufacturers. Once again, the dates in brackets indicate the year in which machines were first sold under the given marque name. As with all of these lists, it is interesting to cross-reference the companies to see their development.

Acme (1902)
A.E.L. (1919)
Alert (1903)
Arden (1912)
Arno (1906)
Atlas (1913)
Aurora (1902)
Beeston (1898)
Birch (1902)
Calcott (1904)
Centaur (1901)
Clarendon (1901)
C.M.M. (1920)

Condor (1907)
Coventry B & D (1923)
Coventry Challenge (1903)
Coventry Eagle (1901)
Coventry Mascot (1922)
Coventry Victor (1919)
Crest (1923)
Croft Cameron (1923)
Dart (1923)
Davison (1902)
DAW (1902)
Dux (1904)
Francis-Barnett (1919)

Globe (1901)
Grindlay Peerless (1923)
G.S.D. (1921)
Hazlewood (1905)
Hobart (1901)
H & R (1922)
Humber (1900)
Invicta (1913)
Kenilworth (1919)
Kingsway (1921)
Lancer (1904)
Lea-Francis (1911)
Marlow (1921)
Mars (1923)
Marseel (1920)
McKechnie (1922)
McKenzie (1921)
Mohawk (1903)
Monopole (1911)
Montgomery (1902)
Morton-Adam (1923)
Newmount (1929)
Omega (1909)
Packman & Poppe (1922)
Pennington (1897)
Powerful (1903)

Premier (1908)
Priory (1919)
Progress (1902)
Revere (1915)
Rex (-Acme) (1900)
Riley (1901)
Rover (1902)
Royal Eagle (1901)
Rudge-Whitworth (1911)
Saxessories (1923)
Singer (1909)
Sparkbrook (1912)
Stafford (1898)
Stan (1919)
Stanley (1902)
Swift (1898)
Townend (1901)
Triumph (1903)
W.D. (1911)
Wee McGregor (1922)
Wheatcroft (1924)
White & Poppe (1902)
White Heather (1903)
Whitley (1902)
Wigan-Barlow (1921)
Williamson (1912)

Early example of the Riley motorcycle

500-c.c. Rudge Tourist Trophy replica from 1930

Early 500-c.c. Centaur

1911 2½-h.p. Singer

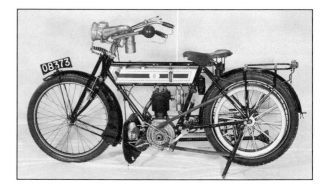

This 1912 Triumph is not the type of machine one associates with the world-famous marque! Most of the well-known Triumphs were built at Meriden many years later.

APPENDIX VI

COMMERCIAL VEHICLE BUILDERS

Daimler double-decker bus built during the Second World War

Designed for rough-terrain work, this Kalmar TT2.6 is one of the many specialized vehicles Kalmar U.K. produce in Coventry.

Early rubber-tyred Maudslay charabanc in service with the Coventry Corporation

Before the First World War there were very few builders of specialist commercial vehicles in the city. Around 1905 George **Iden** became one of the first small manufacturers in Coventry to try his hand at producing lorries and coaches. The venture was short-lived, however, with a production run spanning only two years.

As one would expect, **Daimler** were in right at the start; they are almost a legend in the commercial-vehicle field. In the early days they produced lorries, buses, coaches, ambulances, delivery vans and even tractors. The **Daimler-Renard** name also crops up every now and again. In 1908 Daimler purchased certain patents belonging to the Renard company. Eventually, this part of the long and eventful Daimler story came to an end, their famous buses being one of the last to go. **Jaguar** very nearly revived the tradition by producing a prototype Daimler truck in the early 1960s, but the project came to nothing when Jaguar purchased **Guy Trucks** of Wolverhampton shortly afterwards. Jaguar also bought **Coventry-Climax,** the company famous the world over for their superb fork-lift trucks. Coventry-Climax are now known as **Kalmar,** although their products are still very much the same.

Powered by Riley V-twin engines, several **Lotis** vehicles were produced between 1908 and 1912. These heavier machines were to replace the lightweight **Sturmey** from the same manufacturer.

Maudslay were also making commercials from an early date, lorries, buses and coaches all coming from the Parkside works. Another Parkside-based firm, **Armstrong Siddeley**, built a four-wheel-drive heavy road vehicle to a Pavesi design during the late 1920s. Later on, they would produce light commercials, such as their popular pick-up trucks, on their car chassis, as well as marketing the **Stoneleigh** range of vans, buses and small lorries.

Even **Singer** tried to produce a light mass-produced truck. Several models were introduced during 1929, most powered by 57-h.p. petrol engines, but by 1932 demand had faded, and the company ceased production.

The **Rootes Group** had quite a large interest in the commercial vehicle trade. **Commer** and **Karrier** had a long history in this field, and both marques belonged to Rootes. Between them, they built everything from light vans to tractor/trailer units. Many of their products found service as utility vehicles, being converted to such things as refuse collectors and road-cleaning vehicles. Following the **Sunbeam** takeover, some of the later trucks made under that name were badged as Karrier, though these were not credited to Coventry.

Many coaches and buses also came from Rootes, and several specialists came into being shortly after the Second World War, **Awson, Brooks, Butlins** and **Scott** amongst them. It is also interesting to note that **Carbodies,** famous for

1963 Commer 'walk-through' van. This example was built to police specification by Eagle Engineering of Warwick, and was used by the Warwickshire Constabulary until 1986.

An award-winning Standard Vanguard pick-up

The Armstrong Siddeley railcar in the goods area at Coventry Railway Station just before the Second World War

their London taxi-cabs, diversified slightly in their earlier days to build ambulances – a part of their history rarely recorded.

The **Atlas** range of light commercials was introduced by the **Standard** company around 1958. It consisted mainly of small delivery vans, and was not entirely unsuccessful. Unfortunately, between 1961 and 1963 the vehicles would be badged as **Leylands,** spelling the end of the Atlas. Another name attached to the Standard is that of **Massey-Ferguson,** a firm based in Banner Lane. There they made (and still make) some of the world's best tractors.

Armstrong Siddeley built a 275/300-h.p. V12 petrol engine just before the declaration of the Second World War to use in their so-called Pneumatic Railcars, which ran on rubber tyres. At one stage, the LMS wanted to use them on their network. The reason this didn't happen was that the railmen complained they couldn't hear them coming! **Daimler** produced the same sort of thing at their Radford works in the early 1930s, their vehicle being powered by a large sleeve-valve engine of Daimler's own manufacture.

From trains to boats: incredible though it may seem, Coventry even had a thriving boat-building industry, centred upon the Canal Basin, near the city centre.

Both **Motor Panels** and **Park Sheet Metal** are still involved in commercial vehicle projects. Motor Panels are now the biggest independent truck-cab producers in the world, having bought the American Sheller-Globe concern to complement their operations in Coventry and Wigan. The

The fully engineered Ford Cargo sleeper cab built by Motor Panels proved very popular in the 1980s.

parent company of C.H. Industrials bought Motor Panels in September 1988 from the Rubery Owen organization, and also own Tickford at Bedworth, who recently completed their limited run of Tickford Capris and Ford RS200 competition cars. Park Sheet Metal have had an association with Motor Panels since 1957, and started to produce cab shells. Currently, Freight Rover shells are hand-built at the factory, and several other motor-trade contracts are being filled.

The 1989 GM People Mover. Its four-wheel-drive system was engineered by FF Developments.

APPENDIX VII

MILITARY VEHICLE BUILDERS

ALVIS

Alvis entered the armoured-vehicle industry in 1936. At first, they manufactured the designs of Straussler Mechanisations Ltd, which became Alvis-Straussler and then Alvis Mechanisations Ltd.

Both armoured cars and small tanks were built under this arrangement, but it failed to bring any large-scale production to the Holyhead Road factory, and so, just before the outbreak of the Second World War, Alvis decided to design its own vehicles for the Ministry of Defence.

One of the first Alvis projects was the 'Hefty' gun tractor, but this did not go into production, the L.A.C. taking its place by meeting the requirements of not only a gun tractor, but a light armoured car and general-purpose cross-country vehicle all in one. Ironically, it was the outbreak of war which curtailed any further development!

The Dingo was the last pre-war armoured vehicle built by Alvis. This small scout car was tested against several other products in 1938. Only the Alvis and a Daimler were left in the running, and in the end, the latter won the contest. Oddly, the Dingo name was transferred to the Daimler machine. Bomb-loading trailers were also built at Alvis during this period, and these were used extensively during the war. Even after the hostilities had ended, the company continued to build armoured vehicles. The War Office awarded Alvis a contract to design and develop a range of six-wheeled high-mobility machines. The result was the Saladin, which in turn led to three other vehicles: the Saracen, Salamander and Stalwart, with Rolls-Royce engines and Daimler fluid-flywheel couplings being used in each case.

Looking across a Scorpion tank at some of the six-wheeled fighting vehicles Alvis still build to order. This picture was taken at the Baginton testing-ground during a factory open day.

Scorpion tanks in mid-production. The gun turrets and top armour-plating are lacking.

In the late 1960s Alvis were given a contract to design and build a new 'Combat Vehicle Reconnaissance (Tracked)' by the Ministry of Defence. Powered by a Jaguar XK engine, the Scorpion tank was to become Coventry's most famous modern military product. As with the earlier six-wheeled vehicles, further models were developed from this tank: the Scimitar, Spartan, Strike, Samaritan, Sultan, Samson and Stormer, all of which had different roles on the battlefield.

In 1989 a large order for new tanks was very nearly placed with Alvis, but unfortunately it went to a competitor. Still, there will be others, and with the new generation of tanks (to be known as 'LPXV') already well into development, fresh orders are a certainty.

DAIMLER

During the First World War, many Daimler cars were commandeered and fitted with 'box bodies', the larger models being left as they were and used as staff cars. Several lorries were converted into travelling workshops for use at the Front. Some of the very first tanks were fitted with Daimler engines and transmissions, and these proved to be extremely reliable in service. In the Second World War, the production of Mark I armoured cars and 'Dingo' scout cars was of paramount importance to the Allies. Daimler built nearly 10000 machines of this type.

The Daimler 'Dingo' armoured car

JAGUAR, ROVER AND STANDARD

Jaguar built thousands of trailers with different purposes in the field, as well as special light scout-trucks and side-cars for motorcycles. Only one of each prototype vehicle aimed at replacing the Jeep in parachute drops was ever built, one rear-engined (VA), and the other front-engined (VB). The project was cancelled, as the Jeep was successfully adapted before testing and production got under way.

Rover's most famous military product was the Land Rover, though this was not introduced until 1948, thus missing the war. (It was in any case a Solihull machine.) Several aircraft components were also built at Solihull under the Shadow Factories Scheme.

Standard's contribution to the war was complemented by several light vehicles. The 'Beaverette' light armoured car was introduced in 1940, and was powered by a 14-h.p. engine. This was gradually developed over the war years, with quite a few different versions coming from the works by the end of the hostilites. In 1943 a 12-h.p. cross-country vehicle along the lines of the Jeep was made, though it never went into production. The 'Jungle Bug' was another prototype four-wheel-drive machine, designed like the VA and VB Jaguars with parachute drops in mind. Many vans were also converted for military use.

ROOTES

The total military output from Rootes was quite staggering: armoured cars, armoured reconnaissance vehicles, gun tractors, staff cars (including Monty's famous Humbers), front-line ambulances, troop-carriers, aeroplane-transporters, HQ Staff limousines, fire-engines, vans, four-wheel-drive utility vehicles, heavy transporters adapted for such uses as bridge-girder carriers, double-decker buses, large wagons and refuelling tankers. The Rootes Group were very proud of this tremendous effort, devoting large sections of the wartime in-house magazines to their achievements. Shortly after the war, a four-wheel-drive one-ton truck was also produced for the military. Powered by a Rolls-Royce 4-litre engine, the vehicle was none the less badged and marketed as a Humber.

1942 four-wheel-drive Humber utility vehicle powered by the company's own 4086-c.c. six-cylinder engine.

Monty's 1943 Humber 'Victory Car'

ARMSTRONG SIDDELEY

Siddeley had maintained a good relationship with the R.A.F. for many years, but during the early twenties he tried to expand his business into the Army as well. From 1922 Armstrong Siddeley developed a number of interesting military vehicles, which included some tracked artillery 'Dragons', and their own version of the Italian Pavesi four-wheel-drive, four-wheel-steering tractor. Several air-cooled 350-h.p. tank engines were also supplied to Vickers during 1926, though this side of Armstrong Siddeley was never really the success it was hoped to be.

APPENDIX VIII

THE AIRCRAFT INDUSTRY

This book would not be complete without a mention of the close links between the city's motor and aircraft industries. Coventry is probably just as famous for its flying machines and aero-engines as it is for its cars and cycles. Some items have been listed within the main chapters, but the following is a complete summary of all air-related products to come from the city's factories.

THE SIDDELEY-DEASY MOTOR CAR CO. LTD, later **SIR W.G. ARMSTRONG WHITWORTH AIRCRAFT LTD**
Armstrong-Whitworth of Newcastle combined with the Siddeley-Deasy Motor Co. to form the Armstrong Whitworth Development Co. Ltd, and this in turn was later changed to the Armstrong Siddeley Development Co. Ltd. Many aeroplanes were to come from this famous company, some built to their own design, others produced for other aircraft manufacturers on a subcontract basis.

It was in 1917 that the company received its first contract to build aircraft, the original order being for 100 biplanes known as R.E.7s. The engine fitted to this type of aeroplane was already being built by Siddeley's (the 150-h.p. R.A.F. 4a), so it made a lot of sense to have the complete article built there. This early type of bomber was followed by the R.E.8, a reconnaissance aircraft of which over 1000 were built.

At around the same time, three more aircraft were built at Parkside, two of which were fitted with 200-h.p. Hispano-Suiza engines. These would be designated type R.T.1. The S.R.2, better known as the Siskin, came in 1918. Three of these aircraft were built, the first of which was later fitted with an Armstrong Siddeley 'Jaguar' engine – the name that was the inspiration for Sir William Lyons' company. The Sinaia was also built at Parkside, but only one of four aircraft ordered was ever completed.

The Armstrong Whitworth Tadpole, of 1920 vintage, was an ugly machine built for the Admiralty. Only one of these aircraft was produced, a highly modified D.H.9A. It was during 1920 that the company became known as Sir W.G. Armstrong Whitworth Aircraft Ltd.

The works were moved to Whitley in 1923, and one of the first machines to fly from the new site was the Siskin. (The new Jaguar research and development plant stands on the site of the old Whitley aerodrome.)

Aerial view of the Armstrong Whitworth works at Baginton just before the outbreak of the Second World War

Coventry-built Siskin V fighter aircraft

In 1922 the Siskin II was built, followed shortly afterwards by the Awana troop-carrier. Wolf biplanes were soon put into production, and further improved versions of the Siskin continued to leave the factory.

These were busy times for Whitworth's, Ape, Atlas, Ajax and Argosy aircraft all making their debut within the space of a couple of years. The work-force virtually doubled in size between 1924 and 1927, when a total of over 700 were employed.

The Starling (A.W.14), was first shown at the Olympia Aero Show, but very few of these pretty machines would ever be built. Much more successful was the subsequent project, a passenger plane known as the Atlanta.

Only one of each of the A.W.17, 19 and 23 aircraft was built, and only half a dozen A.W.16s were ever completed. (The missing numbers, incidentally, were given to design proposals that never made it off the drawing-board.) It was during 1928 that the company managed to acquire A.V. Roe Ltd, thus bringing yet another famous name to the city.

The Hawker Hart was also built in Coventry. Its production spread over five years in the city, and totalled over 450 units by the time the run ended in 1937. By now, Siddeley had decided to merge with Hawker Engineering, and a new company was formed, the Hawker-Siddeley Aircraft Co. After the war, it would be known simply as the Hawker-Siddeley Group.

The A.W.27 Ensign was a large passenger aircraft built specially for Imperial Airways and BOAC. At least fifteen

The A.W.27 Ensign was a forty-seater passenger aircraft powered by four 880-h.p. Armstrong Siddeley Tiger IX engines. Designed at Coventry, it was built at Hamble, because space was needed for the Whitley bombers.

were built, and many of them stayed in active service for nearly a decade. The A.W.29 was a one-off, and most of the five Scimitars were sent to Norway.

Production of the Whitley bomber began about three years before the outbreak of the Second World War. By the end of the six-year-long battle, seven different versions and a total of nearly 2000 aircraft had been built. The Albemarle was the next of the Armstrong Whitworth line, and of this over 600 were built.

Whitleys in production at Baginton just before the Second World War, part of the wide-ranging rearmament programme

The Avro Lancaster is possibly Coventry's most famous heavy bomber. The contract for these aircraft was originally given to the company in 1941, but it wasn't until 1943 that the first ones came off the production line. At one time, it was thought that Bristol engines might have to be fitted on the whole Lancaster run, but this was only necessary on the Mark II machines, which were unique to the city. Rolls-Royce Merlin engines were employed on the later versions. A total of 1328 Lancasters were delivered during the war, with its replacement, the Lincoln, overlapping its manufacture towards the end of the hostilities. The Lincoln was later used as a flying testbed for several gas-turbine engines, including the Rolls-Royce Derwent.

Three extraordinary machines left Whitley in the immediate post-war years: the A.W.52G and two experimental A.W.52 aircraft. Extraordinary, yes – but successful? Unfortunately not. These were the code-numbers given to the amazing tailless jet aeroplanes better known as 'flying wings'.

Armstrong Whitworth began making parts for the Gloster Aircraft Co. just after the war. In January 1949 the contract was landed to build Gloster Meteor Mark IVs. The Meteor was Britain's first operational jet aircraft, and was powered by two Rolls-Royce Derwent turbo-jet engines. The Meteor Mark VIII was an improved version of the same basic aeroplane, and production of this model was also carried out in Coventry. Some of these machines were fitted with Armstrong Siddeley Sapphire power units, though fortunately these bore no resemblance to the car engine of the same name!

The 'prone-pilot' Mark VIII was an experimental aircraft built at Baginton to see if the effects of high g-forces could be curbed, but in the end, a successful anti-g flying-suit was developed, giving better results.

Whitworths were responsible for the Meteor Night Fighter project, the first of the series being known as the NF11. The NF12, 13 and 14 followed soon afterwards, with the final development designated TT Mark XX. Production of the latter was confined to the conversion of NF11s. A total of nearly 600 Meteor Night Fighters were built in Coventry, and quite a few of these saw service abroad.

The Apollo was built within the guide-lines of the Brabazon Committee, an organization set up during the war to cater for the need for civil aircraft in the post-war years. Two A.W.55 Apollo aircraft were built; one first flew in 1949, the other in 1952, but these were to be the first and last of the type, as they were thought to be too small from a commercial point of view. With a tapered body, stretching the machine would not have been easy, and the company refused to try. Vickers, on the other hand, slightly lengthened their Viscount aircraft, and gained many hundreds of orders at Armstrong Whitworth's expense.

The Sea Hawk was the first Hawker jet fighter to go into production, and this too was built in Coventry. After just thirty-five were manufactured at Hawker, it was decided that

The Midland Air Museum's beautifully restored Sea Hawk

both construction and any further development should be undertaken by Whitworth's. A single Rolls-Royce Nene turbo-jet powered this elegant aeroplane, and the first Coventry-built Sea Hawk flew at the end of 1952. Several versions were made before the last one left the factory, but in the meantime, Hawker had introduced the Rolls-Royce Avon-powered Hunter. Their production overlapped, as the first Hunters began to be put together early in 1954. As with the Gloster Meteor Mark VIII, sometimes the Armstrong Siddeley Sapphire engine was fitted.

The Gloster Javelin was to be the last aircraft Armstrong Whitworth built under subcontract. Two Siddeley Sapphire engines were mounted side by side, and in all, nine versions of the Javelin were produced. It was a fairly important aircraft in that it was the first delta-winged aeroplane to go into service wth the R.A.F. The first Javelin flight was in November 1951, but production at Coventry did not begin until 1956. Just two years later, the 133rd and last aircraft flew away.

In 1959, a merger took place between the Hawker-Siddeley Group and its one-time major rival, Bristol, and a new company called Bristol-Siddeley was formed. The Argosy was the last Armstrong Whitworth aircraft, and indeed, the last aircraft to be built in Coventry by any manufacturer. This large freight-carrying aeroplane was originally destined for military use, but as the project progressed, the specification was gradually aimed more at the civil operator. The A.W.650 Argosy was the original version (also known as the 100 series), with the 200 series following five years later, in 1964. The 660 (Armstrong Whitworth Argosy C Mark I) was also built during this time, bringing the project full circle, as this was to be a military machine. However, 1966 was to spell the end for this delightful range of aircraft, for this is when the last of them left the works.

The Armstrong Siddeley Cougar aero-engine was the company's last piston engine, and had an international rating of 690 h.p. The Cougar was soon overtaken by prop-jet engines.

The company were also responsible for many aero-engines as well as complete aircraft. Their first projects were the R.A.F. 1A V8 90-h.p. and V12 140-h.p. units, but they soon built their own world-famous Puma engine. The Jaguar followed shortly afterwards, as did the Lynx, Mongoose, Genet, Panther and Cheetah, the last of these totalling well over 40000 units in service.

HUMBER and THE ROOTES GROUP

During 1910 and 1911 the Humber company built several different mono- and biplanes, the Humber-Lovelace, Humber-Le Blon and Blériot being fairly typical examples. The company's engines at this time consisted of a three-cylinder radial 30-h.p. unit, and a four-cylinder version rated at 50 h.p. The aircraft department continued to be kept busy throughout the First World War, when many Avros left the Humber works.

Rootes gained their first order for aero-engines in February 1937. This was for 200 units, and it was placed by the Bristol Co. Because of the Shadow Factories Scheme, the group had their own Aero-Engine and Airframe departments, as well as multi-cell test houses and a superb reconditioning plant. By the time the Second World War came to an end, Rootes had built one in seven of the United Kingdom's total output of bombers, and had dealt with more than 21000 different engines.

STANDARD

Standard built B.E.12s at their new Canley factory during the early part of the First World War, after obtaining an original War Office contract for fifty aircraft. Unfortunately, the B.E.12 proved to be unsatisfactory in battle, so Sopwith Pups took their place on the production lines late in 1916. The equally famous R.E.8s were later built alongside these aircraft.

In mid-1918 Standard were given a large order to build Bristol F.2B fighter planes, though by the time the first of these was completed, the war had ended, and all of them, along with the final few Pups and R.E.8s, were delivered only to go straight into storage. In the following year, around 300 Buzzards were built, but far larger numbers of aircraft would come from the Standard company during the next war.

After the Second World War was declared, the company got back down to building aeroplanes for the Ministry. Oxford Trainers and Gypsy Moths were built, but by far the most famous Standard product of the war years was the De Havilland Mosquito fighter-bomber, of which 1066 left the factory. Around 3000 Beaufighter fuselages were made, over 20000 Bristol Hercules aero-engines, and literally thousands of related parts. For his contribution to the war effort, John Black received a knighthood.

JAGUAR

Although Jaguar didn't build any complete aircraft, they manufactured many parts for both the Whitley bomber, Meteor III, Short Stirling, Mosquito and Spitfire. They also made Cheetah engine parts, and had a heavily used service and repair department.

Humber aircraft about to set off on an air race. c.1910

MESSRS J. SHAW

This company built the infamous Flying Fox of 1892. Powered by a 3-h.p. electric motor, and weighing in at 700 lb, the machine failed even to get off the ground. At least they had a go!

ALVIS

After the declaration of the First World War, a French Gnome Rhone rotary engine was sent to Daimler with a view to manufacturing it at Coventry. Drawings were made up in just over a week, ready for an English version to be built.

T.G. John of the Alvis company purchased a licence to build Gnome radial engines in 1935, and a new and modern factory was built so that production could commence five months later. A further building, the test house at Baginton, was erected shortly afterwards. Alvis held licences to modify, develop and build (in descending order of size) the 1500-h.p. Alcides, the Alcides Major, the Pelides and the Pelides Major. The smallest Alvis engine of the time was known as the Maeonides Major.

The Alvis-designed Leonides was a natural progression from the previous power units that the company had worked on. Leonides was a single-row engine introduced just before the war. Further development was postponed until around 1944, when the factory was more concerned with making components for the famous Rolls-Royce Kestrel and Merlin engines. They also had a contract to service and repair these units.

The larger Leonides Major came later, and both were to be employed on several well-known aircraft. Helicopters also started to use adapted units towards the end of the 1950s, and the original Saunders-Roe hovercraft was also fitted with a Leonides engine. The last one was built in 1970, by which time around 2300 had left the factory. Several other products continued to keep the works busy, but none was successful enough to be developed any further.

In 1989 Alvis were working on a gas-turbine engine to be used as an auxiliary power unit, and it was hoped that the R.A.F. would order many of these engines for use in their aircraft. In the meantime, a contract with Boeing for flap gearboxes kept the company in constant touch with the industry.

W.O. BENTLEY

Bentley, although more famous for his exceptional sporting cars, started his long engineering career by redesigning the Clerget rotary engine. When the First World War broke out, Bentley took his ideas on aluminium pistons to the Admiralty, who in turn persuaded both Rolls-Royce and Sunbeam to incorporate this feature into their engines.

Through the extensive use of aluminium, Bentley's BR1 and BR2 engines became far lighter, more powerful and

The nine-cylinder Alvis Leonides aero-engine

Power output of the Alvis gas turbine being measured on a test-bed

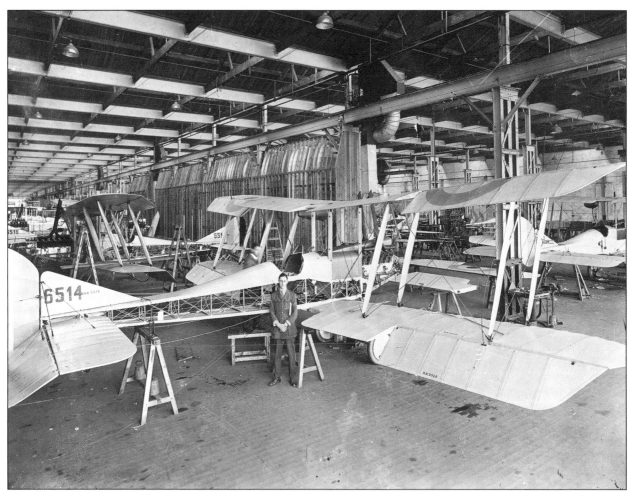

Aircraft production at the Daimler works

Coventry's last aircraft, the Armstrong Whitworth Argosy

more reliable than previous units of this type. A lot of the work was carried out at the Humber factory, with testing taking place at Parkside. Humber eventually went on to build the Bentley engines, which were fitted to such well-known Sopwith aircraft as the Camel, the Snipe and, later, the Salamander.

ROLLS-ROYCE

The subject of Rolls-Royce aero-engines is so vast that it merits a book on its own; indeed, several volumes have already been written. With Rolls-Royce engines, listing the Coventry-built ones poses several problems, as more often than not parts were manufactured at the Crewe works, with a final assembly taking place elsewhere.

The Mamba, Olympus, Sapphire and Viper were definitely Coventry projects. However, the Pegasus, RB-199 and RB-211 power units also had strong links with the city. Many applications were found for these superb engines, regarded as being some of the best in the world.

GLOVER

The ever-inventive Glover brothers also tried to build an aircraft. Their intention was to enter it for the *Daily Mail* challenge for the first flying machine to cross the Channel, a prize of £10000 being offered. The Glover aircraft was powered by an early FN four-cylinder motorcycle engines. The wings were found to be inadequate, and the machine was pushed back from the top of Barras Lane into the workshop for further alterations. In 1909, however, Blériot flew across the Channel, and the Glovers abandoned their project.

DAIMLER

Daimler's involvement in the aero industry came about during the First World War, when the Allies became desperately short of aircraft after the first two years of fighting. Although Daimler had no previous experience in the field, the Ministry of War asked the company to build the 80-h.p. Gnome engine under licence (*see* Alvis, *above*). The first British example of the engine was running in only eight weeks, an achievement that would be hard to match even with the high technology of today.

The Ministry were sufficiently pleased with the results to issue a contract to build complete aircraft as well, and on receipt of the order Daimler began building their own aerodrome on the Radford estate. An engine based on a Renault design (R.A.F.1) went into production, and later the Bentley BR2 was developed at the Daimler works. Around 1245 of these engines were produced during the last six months of the hostilities.

The Bristol Aero Co. awarded Daimler a private contract to produce some 400 different aero-engine components towards the end of the 1920s, and the arrangement continued, further contracts being added, right through to the Second World War.

Rolls-Royce approached Daimler during the war to arrange for the manufacture of several large machined parts of Rolls-Royce engines. When the war drew to a close, a total of around 50000 Hercules, Mercury and Pegasus engines had been added to the already massive list of Daimler's manufacturing achievements, as well as the so-called 'power egg' units that were produced in the shadow factories.

After the war, Daimler were in no position to maintain their links with the aircraft industry, and thus reverted to their mainstream activities of quality motor-vehicle production.

Of course, many thousands of components and armaments were produced by the **Coventry Ordnance Works**, but a total of 710 aircraft were also built there. R.E.8 aircraft were manufactured at the Burlington Carriage works during the First World War, and (as mentioned earlier) **Singer** produced several hundred aero-engines over the same period. The manufacture of aircraft components is still quite an important trade for the Coventry engineering shops; **Clarke, Cluley & Co.** have supplied Westland helicopters with parts for some years, **Cornercroft Engineering** and **J.S. Chinn** rely heavily on the industry, and there are many other firms who carry out smaller contract work.

INDEX

References to illustrations are in italics